COOKING WITH
BREAD

COOKING WITH BREAD

By William I. Kaufman

Published in association with Ward Foods, Inc.

CORINTHIAN EDITIONS, INC.
New York
1969

Book design and drawings by The Corchia Group, Inc.

Library of Congress catalog card number: 73–81773

PREFACE

"A loaf of bread ... and thou"—these are the two main ingredients in all the delightful recipes that are contained between the covers of this unique cook book. In fact you will seldom need a whole loaf of bread. Often a cup, or less, of crumbs will do the trick. But the point is that bread, in some form—crumbs, cubes, slices—is a necessary part of every recipe.

Stay your hand the next time you start to toss away the crusts trimmed from sandwiches, the ends or "heels" of a loaf, or a few dry slices. Keep two or three jars with tight-fitting lids nearby. Dry out or toast the crumbs or cubes; toast the slices, too, crumble them and store them in the jars in the refrigerator until you are ready to prepare, say, Baked Sea Food Newburg (page 52), which calls for two-thirds of a cup, or Potato Croquettes (page 85), which needs three-fourths cup, or even Friday Night Chicken (page 37), which may require all you have stored away, or even more.

The second main ingredient is *you*. It is up to you to remember that when you throw away edible bread you throw away food value as well as money. Food value, because today's enriched bread supplies many elements vital to good nutrition as well as calories for energy. Money, because bread is no longer five cents a loaf!

The recipes that follow range from simple family dishes, such as Stuffed Cabbage Leaves (page 15), Meat Loaf Rouge (page 13), and Fancy Franks (page 7), to epicurean treats for company like Hula Chicken (page 26), or Party Veal Cutlets (page 17).

You are going to enjoy this book. Be sure to read the introduction with its fascinating history of bread down through the ages. Then browse through the recipes, making a mental or written note of one or two you want to try right away. You will then be embarked on an interesting trip in the world of cookery. And we wager you'll never throw away another crust!

Beth Merriman
Food Editor *Parade*

CONTENTS

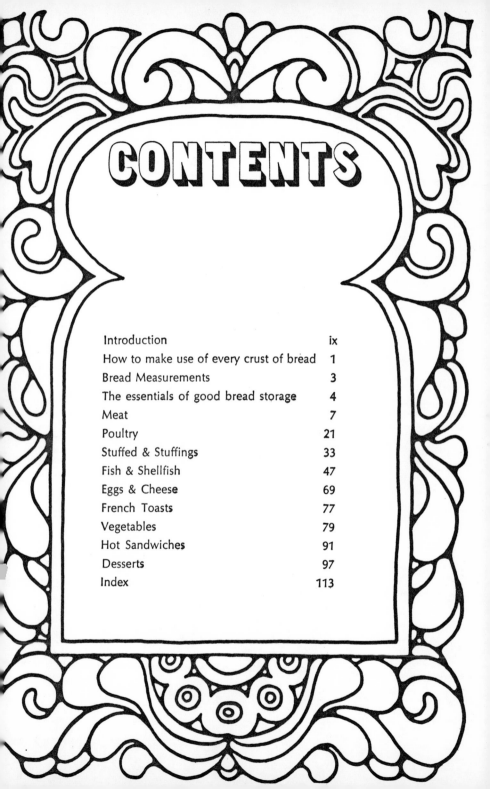

INTRODUCTION

THE STAFF OF LIFE

The history of bread is the story of civilization itself, and each day scientists continue to reveal new and interesting facts about one of our oldest and most important foods. Their findings tell us why man, since primitive days, has demanded bread as part, if not all, of his daily fare.

Research has proved that early men kept themselves alive by eating wild grains along the trails and in the underbrush while they hunted for meat. When they discovered that they could plant and cultivate the seeds of wild grain, they realized that a nomadic existence was no longer necessary and banded together in a common effort for survival, depending less on the vagaries of the huntsman's life. At first the seeds must have been eaten raw, but archeological discoveries indicate that, in the Stone Age, the Swiss Lake Dwellers produced a flat loaf, the analysis of which shows that the bread was made from coarsely ground flour that was hard on the outside and had a soft interior. We deduce that primitive man had discovered the principles of mixing flour with water and that he poured the mixture on heated stones to bake it.

The same means of baking bread prevailed through the ancient civilizations of Babylonian Chaldea, Assyria, and Egypt. Bread in Egypt was placed in the tomb with the deceased so that the combined spiritual body and soul, the Ka, would have food enough to supply energy for the trip to heaven.

In early Egypt every village had its public ovens and each noble his private bakery to supply him with fresh bread. By the time of the Pharaohs two kinds of bread, leavened and unleavened, were in use.

In view of the limited amount of bread misguided moderns eat for fear of gaining weight, it is interesting to note that the Egyptian housewife served her husband three small loaves of leavened bread each meal, and she herself ate nearly as much. Yet all ancient drawings and artifacts show the ancient Egyptians to have been strikingly slender and graceful.

The recipe for the common flat bread of the Nile seems to have been a mixture of water, flour and sugar. When the dough was set aside, wild yeast cells in the air probably settled on it. The yeast spores combined with and fermented the sugar, and air bubbles formed, causing pockets that expanded the dough. Heat from the baking stones added to this rising action; when the bread cooled it retained its height.

Such bread was first baked on flat stones, but later the enterprising Egyptians discovered that a better-tasting bread could be baked in a heavy clay jar set in hot coals. The jar had a lower section for the fire. The upper section for the bread was open at the top. This was the earliest example of a bread oven.

The Phoenicians carried this earthenware oven to Greece, and in 600 B.C. the first beehive oven was fabricated as an improvement on the Egyptian model. The beehive was kettle shaped and had excellent qualities of heat retention. At about this time the Greeks developed the first mill in which large quantities of flour could be ground. It was called the "hourglass" and contained a bin or hopper into which grain was poured. Below were two stones that moved against each other, crushing the grain as it fell. First men, then animals, were harnessed to activate the mechanism, and finally a small hand-operated version was invented for Grecian home use.

As the Roman Empire absorbed Greece and Grecian invention, the Romans developed a baking industry, adapting the oven and the mill to their own needs. They bricked over the beehive, completely enclosing the baking chambers, thickening the walls to hold the heat more effectively and adding a chimney to carry off the smoke. As for the mill, the Romans found water to be a more efficient source of power and harnessed it to turn a wheel to which they attached small paddles. An axle extending from the wheel activated the grinding stones. White flour extracted from mills of this kind greatly resembled our white flour of today, and the men who produced it were so important to the Roman economy that legislation regulating their trade in 200 B.C. made them virtual civil servants.

In the 12th century the windmill was devised. A bakers guild was formed, and the industry became so important in the Middle Ages that standards of bread quality and rules for employment were established.

For all Europeans bread became the holiest of edibles. It was revered as the symbol of the Redeemer's body. If it fell to the floor it was kissed and carefully wiped off before it was eaten.

By the middle of the 13th century bakers were so prominent and so highly considered that some became mayors or judges and many served on governing councils. One of the most famous medieval laws, the English Assize of Bread, was enacted during this period. Issued in 1266, the statute set the price of bread and established a definite weight for each loaf. The Assize remained in force for six centuries and was still in force when the Jamestown colonists brought the art of bread making to America in 1604. By 1640 commercial bakeries were already in operation even though they had to brave competition from the Colonial homemakers.

Bread "hard as flint" fortified the pioneers as they opened the West, and as America grew the baking industry kept pace. For the first time in history the "white bread of kings" was available to rich and poor alike, although sectional tastes prevailed for a short time, with the South clinging to its love of corn bread and rural New Englanders sticking to their preferred "rye and Injun" loaves.

Bread baking followed along the lines of Roman habit until the industrialization of the United States after 1850, when new improvements in oven construction and trough manufacture brought on the development of a broader range of baked goods. In the last half of the 19th century bakers made bread, to be sure, but they also baked crackers, cookies, biscuits, pies and cakes and they are still doing so.

The Ward Baking Company, forerunner of Ward Foods, Inc., a pioneer in the baking industry, is credited with being the first to erect and operate a modern, sanitary bakery (Pittsburgh, in 1903). It was the first baking company to establish a Baking Research Fellowship (The Mellon Institute, Pittsburgh, in 1909), and in 1911 Ward was the first baking company to abandon the use of horse-drawn delivery vehicles, thus doing away with unsanitary stables hitherto part of or adjacent to bakeries.

Today, with general public acceptance, the bakery industry is one of our largest food-processing enterprises, and bread is a precision product in which every ingredient is accurately weighed before it is utilized. These ingredients are turned into a mixer and stirred mechanically until the proper consistency and tested temperature are achieved. Then the dough is poured into troughs and placed in a warm room to rise. Afterwards it is apportioned into individual loaves by scaling and dividing machines. Next the dough passes to the rounder, then to the molder, and finally into the baking pans, which are conducted through the proofing boxes where the dough is again given a chance to rise. At last the pans reach the ovens which are maintained at the most accurate temperatures possible. When the loaves are fully baked they are ready to be sliced and securely wrapped for market.

Nearly all the white bread we eat is enriched with vitamins and minerals. Cooperating with medical and nutritional authorities, the bakers and millers of America have contributed strongly to the decrease in deficiency diseases and have made a great contribution to general health in America by restoring to bread the thiamine, riboflavin, niacin and iron reduced in the milling process without changing the quality, appearance, or flavor of the breads we enjoy so much. The U.S. Public Health Service, noting the almost complete decline of beriberi and pellagra in the nation, has stated that the most important change in nutrition in recent years is the increase in the intake of thiamine and niacin (both B vitamins) due to enrichment of flour and bread. Enrichment is now a permanent part of American life, with roots so strong they are spreading to other countries.

Penny for penny, today's modern loaf of enriched white bread furnishes more than its fair share of nutrients needed in a balanced diet. For five cents you can purchase five slices of bread that supply nine grams of protein, while the same five cents can only purchase six grams of protein in milk, seven grams of protein in eggs or eight grams of protein in meat.

Bread is delicious, nutritious and inexpensive, and its use in these recipes will show that it is also one of the most versatile, adaptable and easily procurable comestibles known to man.

It continues to be what it has been through the ages—the staff of life.

WILLIAM I. KAUFMAN

How to make use of every crust of bread

Soft bread cubes

Stack 2 or 3 slices of fresh bread on a bread board; with a sharp knife, using a sawing motion, cut sliced bread into strips of desired width. Cut again in opposite direction to form cubes of even size. USES: Casserole garnish. Stuffings for meat fish poultry and vegetable dishes. Hot cheese dishes. Combined with garlic and oil and added to salads. Puddings and muffins.

Soft bread crumbs

Tear a fresh slice of bread into small pieces with the fingers, or use electric blender. USES: Stuffings for meat, fish, poultry and vegetable dishes. Combined with eggs before frying. Combined with main ingredient as filler. Puddings.

Toasted bread cubes

Arrange soft bread cubes on a cookie sheet. Place cookie sheet under a preheated broiler or in a slow oven and toast until cubes are golden brown on all sides, turning occasionally. USES: Croutons. Mixed into salads. Garnish for casseroles.

Dry bread crumbs

Grind dry bread through a food chopper, using fine blade, or use electric blender. Tie a paper bag on the blade end of grinder so that the crumbs will drop into bag as they are ground. If fine bread crumbs are desired, sift the crumbs through a sieve. Store coarse dry and fine dry crumbs in separate covered containers. USES: Add to barbecue sauces for basting. Stuffings for meat, poultry, fish and vegetable dishes. Casserole dishes. Sprinkle over dishes before browning in oven. For frying meat, fish, poultry and vegetables after dipping into egg or alone. Puddings. Combined with fruits for pie topping.

Buttered bread crumbs

⅓ cup butter or margarine   **1 cup dry bread crumbs**

Melt butter in frypan. When hot, add bread crumbs. Stir constantly until crumbs are golden brown. USES: Sprinkle over meat, fish, poultry and vegetable dishes that are to be baked.

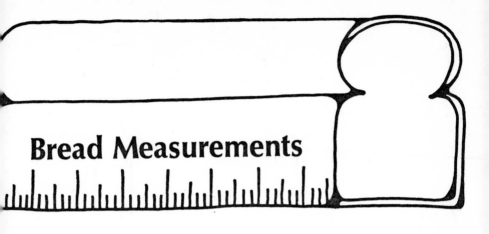

Bread Measurements

1 slice (5/8 inch) fresh enriched bread yields approximately 1 cup soft bread cubes.

1 slice (5/8 inch) fresh enriched bread yields approximately 1 cup soft bread crumbs.

1 slice (5/8 inch) fresh enriched bread yields approximately 3/4 cup toasted or dry bread cubes.

1 slice (5/8 inch) dry enriched bread yields approximately 1/3 cup dry bread crumbs.

1 package (10 ounces) toasted bread crumbs yields approximately 3 1/2 cups.

1 package (8 ounces) stuffing mix yields approximately 3 cups.

The Essentials
of good bread storage

Bread deserves good treatment. It is perishable, and the way in which it is stored affects its good eating qualities. Wrapping and storage conditions are factors in maintaining freshness. Signs of staling are loss of flavor and aroma of fresh bread, and increasing firmness.

ALWAYS WRAP AT THE START

In the modern bakery, bread is scientifically wrapped in moisture-resistant material. This is the best procedure for maintaining freshness because it keeps the bread in an ideal, humid atmosphere. Wrapped bread or packaged rolls should be left in original wrappers when placed in storage units. Bread and rolls purchased unwrapped should be enclosed in moisture-vaporproof papers or moisture-resistant bags before storing. When serving bread or when making sandwiches, remove only as many slices as needed. Fold the excess wrapping material over the remaining bread to retain moisture and to exclude airborne mold spores. Hard- or crisp-crusted breads and rolls should be eaten fresh immediately upon purchase.

BE WISE ABOUT STORAGE AREAS

Refrigerator: Bread may be stored in the refrigerator to retard mold growth, especially during hot weather, but the longer the refrigeration period, the firmer bread becomes. Refrigeration temperatures step up staling, and the use of wrappers or special containers do not offset these effects of cool temperature on bread freshness.

Freezer: Bread should be stored in frozen-food cabinets at 0°F. or lower. These temperatures keep the flavor, freshness, original moisture and aroma of bread intact if it is wrapped securely in moisture-vapor-proof material beforehand. Bread, thawed or fresh, stales at the same rate under like storage conditions. Fresh hard- or crisp-crusted breads or rolls should be wrapped loosely in kraft paper. To use, unwrap and thaw bread at room temperature. Heat, uncovered, in a hot oven for about 5 minutes and serve immediately. Freezing stale or partially stale bread will not restore its freshness.

Bread Box: Properly wrapped bread may be stored satisfactorily at room temperature in a clean, dry, ventilated storage unit, container or drawer. Increased ventilation of the unit should be allowed for during hot weather. Such units should be placed away from all heat-producing equipment such as ranges and radiators. Temperatures above 80°F. foster mold growth. Containers used for storage of bread should be thoroughly washed weekly. Baking soda dissolved in warm water is the preferred agent for odorless cleaning. The unit should be dried well, including all joinings, and it should be free of crumbs. Any remaining moisture or crumbs may favor mold growth.

MEAT

Fancy Franks

2 tablespoons chopped
   onion
1 cup fine-chopped celery
2 tablespoons shortening
½ teaspoon salt
⅛ teaspoon pepper

⅛ teaspoon poultry seasoning or ground sage
½ cup milk
3 cups coarse bread
   crumbs, toasted
10 frankfurters
10 bacon slices

Cook onion and celery in shortening in frypan until tender. Combine onion, celery, salt, pepper, poultry seasoning, milk and toasted crumbs and mix well. Split frankfurters lengthwise almost through to bottom. Spoon stuffing into frankfurters. Wrap 1 bacon slice around each frankfurter. Fasten with food picks. Place frankfurters on a rack in a shallow roasting pan. Bake in a hot oven (400°F.) for 25 to 30 minutes, or until bacon is cooked.

Yield: 4 to 6 servings

Vegetable and Sausage Casserole

1 pound sausage meat
2 tablespoons minced
  onion
¼ cup chopped pimiento
⅛ teaspoon pepper
1 teaspoon dry mustard
1 teaspoon salt, divided
1 package (10 ounces)
  frozen mixed vegetables,
  or 1 cup grated process
  cheese

12 slices of enriched bread,
  crusts removed
6 eggs, beaten
3 cups milk
2 teaspoons
  Worcestershire sauce
6 strips of pimiento
4 slices of stuffed
  green olives

Cook sausage meat in a large frypan over medium heat until lightly browned, stirring with a fork to break into small pieces. Drain off excess fat. Add onion, chopped pimiento, pepper, mustard and half of salt. Cook vegetables according to package directions until barely tender. Drain and add to sausage. Cool. Arrange half of bread slices in a greased oblong baking dish (8 x 12 inches). Spread sausage mixture over bread. Top with remaining bread slices. Cover closely and refrigerate, overnight if desired.

To complete casserole, combine beaten eggs, milk, remaining salt and Worcestershire sauce. Pour over casserole and let stand for about 10 minutes. Set baking dish in a pan of hot water and bake in a slow oven (325°F.) for 1¼ hours, or until nicely browned. Garnish with pimiento strips and olive slices arranged to resemble a poinsettia.

Yield: 6 servings

Note: If cheese is substituted for vegetables, add it to the sausage and arrange it over bread slices.

To announce that their bread was ready for sale, 14th-century bakers blew loud blasts on horns.

Sausage, Hominy and Tomato Scramble

1 pound bulk pork sausage
½ cup fine dry bread crumbs
⅔ cup undiluted
  evaporated milk
¾ teaspoon ground sage,
  divided
¼ cup flour

1 can (1 pound, 4
  ounces) hominy,
  drained
2 cans (1 pound each)
  stewed tomatoes
1 teaspoon salt
Dash of pepper

Combine sausage, crumbs, evaporated milk and ½ teaspoon sage. Divide mixture into 16 portions and form into balls. Roll in flour to coat, saving remaining flour for later. Begin cooking gently in a cold frypan. Continue cooking, turning to brown lightly on all sides. Dip off all but 2 to 3 tablespoons fat. Blend in reserved flour, then add vegetables, salt pepper and remaining ¼ teaspoon sage; mix well. Cover and cook over low heat for 15 minutes, or until thickened.
Yield: 6 to 8 servings

Lamb Breast with Carrot Stuffing

2½ tablespoons melted
  drippings or shortening
2¼ cups soft ½-inch
  bread cubes
¾ cup fine-shredded
  raw carrot
6 tablespoons minced
  onion

2 eggs, beaten
¾ teaspoon salt
¼ cup hot bouillon
1 lamb breast with
  pocket and cracked
  bones (about 2
  pounds)

Combine drippings, soft bread cubes, carrot, onion, beaten eggs and salt. Add bouillon and mix well. Fill pocket in lamb breast with stuffing. Place in a shallow pan, with breast ribs down, and bake in a slow oven (300°F.) for about 1 hour and 45 minutes, until meat is tender.
Yield: 4 servings

Lamb Steaks with Curried Fruit Stuffing

1½ tablespoons shortening
6 lamb shoulder steaks
   or chops
Dash of salt
Dash of pepper
½ cup fine-chopped celery
½ cup fine-chopped onion
1 quart soft ½-inch
   bread cubes

½ teaspoon curry
   powder
½ cup seedless raisins,
   plumped
¼ cup peach juice
6 peach halves
¼ cup sifted brown
   sugar, divided

Melt shortening in large frypan. Season lamb steaks on both sides with salt and pepper, then brown them on both sides in the shortening. Place in a shallow baking pan. Sauté celery and onion in the pan drippings, then combine them with soft bread cubes, curry powder, plumped raisins and peach juice. Place about ½ cup stuffing on top of each chop. Top stuffing with a peach half, rounded side up. Sprinkle about 1½ teaspoons brown sugar over each peach. Bake, uncovered, in a moderate oven (350°F.) for 30 minutes.
Yield: 6 servings.

Char-Broiled Stuffed Pork Chops

1 quart soft ½-inch
   enriched bread cubes
1⅓ tablespoons minced
   onion
¼ cup fine-chopped celery
¼ teaspoon pepper

1 teaspoon salt
1 teaspoon dried dill
   seeds
⅓ cup hot water
6 double pork chops,
   with pockets

Combine soft bread cubes, onion, celery, pepper, salt and dill seeds. Toss to blend. Gradually blend in hot water. Fill the pocket in each chop with about ⅓ cup stuffing. Fasten edges of chop together with skewers. Broil over medium-hot coals for about 1 hour, or until chops are browned and thoroughly done. Turn several times during cooking.
Yield: 6 servings

Pirate's Treasure Pork Chop

¼ cup chopped celery
¼ cup chopped onion
2 tablespoons shortening
1 egg, slightly beaten
¼ cup water
¼ teaspoon salt
2 teaspoons poultry
  seasoning
2 cups coarse bread
  crumbs, toasted

½ cup fine-chopped
  cashews
6 pork rib chops, cut
  1½ inches thick,
  with pockets
3 tablespoons lard or
  drippings
1 can (10½ ounces)
  condensed mushroom
  soup
½ cup water

Cook celery and onion in 2 tablespoons shortening until tender
Combine egg, water, salt, poultry seasoning, celery, onion, toasted
bread crumbs and chopped cashews. Mix well. Fill pockets in pork
chops with stuffing. Brown in 3 tablespoons lard or drippings in large
frypan. Pour off drippings. Mix mushroom soup and water and pour
over chops. Cover tightly and simmer for 1 hour, or until done.
Yield: 6 servings

Beef Stroganoff

¼ cup flour
¾ teaspoon salt
1½ pounds beef, cut into
  1-inch cubes
3 tablespoons shortening

½ cup sliced small
  onions
⅓ cup water
1 cup dairy sour cream
¼ teaspoon paprika

Combine flour and salt. Roll each cube of meat in flour. Melt shortening
in a skillet. Add onions and beef and brown on all sides. Add ⅓ cup
water. Cover tightly and cook slowly for 1 hour, or until tender. Blend
sour cream and paprika. Add to cooked meat during last 10 minutes of
cooking time. Serve in Bread Stuffing Ring* (see following page).

Bread Stuffing Ring

2½ quarts ½-inch soft
 bread cubes
1½ teaspoons salt
½ teaspoon dried marjoram
¼ teaspoon dried rosemary

¼ cup melted
 shortening
1 egg, beaten
¾ cup water
¾ cup chopped celery

Combine soft bread cubes, salt, marjoram, rosemary, shortening, beaten egg, water and celery. Pack stuffing into a greased 1½-quart ring mold. Bake in a moderate oven (350°F.) for 30 minutes.
Yield: 3½ cups Beef Stroganoff   6 cups stuffing   6 servings

Pacific Favorite Casserole

8 ounces dried beef
1 cup diced celery
1 cup diced onion
2 tablespoons shortening
2 tablespoons flour
2 cups milk
¼ teaspoon pepper
½ cup grated American
 cheese

1 can (4½ ounces)
 chopped ripe olives
4 ounces wide egg
 noodles, cooked,
 seasoned, drained
⅓ cup coarse bread
 crumbs, toasted
1 tablespoon melted
 butter

Cut dried beef into pieces, if desired. Cook celery and onion in shortening in a saucepan until tender. Stir in flour. Add milk and cook, stirring constantly, until thickened. Add pepper. Remove sauce from heat. Add grated cheese and stir until melted. Add dried beef and ripe olives. Combine noodles with dried-beef mixture and pour into a greased 2-quart casserole. Mix toasted crumbs and butter and sprinkle over meat mixture. Bake in a moderate oven (350°F.) for 30 minutes.
Yield: 6 servings

The European "napkins" of the 12th century were made of dough. After they became soaked with wine and soup they were eaten by the diners.

Best-Ever Beef Roll-Ups

1 beef round steak, cut
½ inch thick
¼ pound pork sausage
½ pound ground beef
1 cup soft bread crumbs
2 tablespoons minced onion
2 tablespoons minced
parsley
¼ teaspoon curry powder
¼ teaspoon garlic salt
¼ cup flour
3 tablespoons
shortening
1 can (10¼ ounces)
condensed beef
consommé
2 tablespoons ketchup

Cut steak into 5 or 6 portions and pound each piece until it is ¼ inch thick. Mix together sausage, ground beef, bread crumbs, onion, parsley, curry powder and garlic salt. Place about ¼ cup meat-crumb mixture on each piece of steak and roll like a jelly roll. Fasten with food picks or skewers. Dredge beef rolls with flour. Brown meat rolls slowly in shortening or drippings in large frypan. Pour off drippings. Combine consommé and ketchup and add to meat. Cover tightly and cook slowly for 1½ hours, or until meat is tender. Thicken cooking liquid for gravy, if desired.
Yield: 5 to 6 servings

Meat Loaf Rouge

2 pounds ground beef
chuck
½ pound pork sausage
1½ cups dry bread crumbs
1 egg
2 teaspoons salt
¼ teaspoon pepper
1 onion, chopped
1 cup tomato juice

Mix all ingredients together in a mixing bowl. Place in a loaf pan (9 x 5 x 3 inches) and bake in a moderate oven (350°F.) for 2 to 2½ hours. Baste during baking with additional tomato juice.
Yield: 8 servings

South Seas Meatballs

1 cup soft bread crumbs
1 teaspoon salt
⅛ teaspoon pepper
½ cup chopped onion,
  divided
½ cup milk
1 tablespoon soy sauce,
  divided
1 pound ground beef
¼ cup sugar
1½ tablespoons cornstarch
¼ teaspoon ground ginger

1 cup pineapple juice
2 tablespoons vinegar
1 tablespoon butter
  or margarine
1 can (8 ounces)
  water chestnuts,
  drained and cut into
  ¼-inch slivers
2 cans (1 pound each)
  bean sprouts
1 cup coarsely chopped
  green pepper

Combine bread crumbs, salt, pepper, ¼ cup onion, milk, 2 teaspoons soy sauce and ground beef. Form into 16 balls, using about 2 tablespoons of mixture for each ball. Place in a shallow baking pan and bake in a moderate oven (350°F.) until browned, about 30 minutes. Combine sugar, cornstarch and ginger in a saucepan. Add pineapple juice, vinegar, remaining soy sauce and butter. Cook over low heat, stirring constantly, until thickened. Add water chestnuts and reheat. Combine bean sprouts, remaining onion and green pepper in frypan. Simmer until onion is tender. Drain off liquid. Spoon bean-sprout mixture onto plates, top with meatballs, and pour sauce over all.
Yield: 4 to 5 servings

Layered Meat Loaf

1 pound ground beef
1 pound ground veal
½ pound ground pork
2 eggs, divided
½ cup fine dry bread crumbs
½ cup milk
3 teaspoons salt, divided

⅛ teaspoon pepper
1 cup soft ½-inch
  bread cubes
2 tablespoons melted
  butter
1 pimiento, chopped
½ cup chopped celery

Combine meats, 1 egg, bread crumbs, milk, 2½ teaspoons salt, and pepper in mixing bowl. Pack half of meat mixture in a loaf pan (9 x 5 x 3 inches). Combine bread cubes, remaining 1 egg, butter, pimiento, celery and remaining ½ teaspoon salt; press on top of meat mixture. Top with remaining half of meat. Bake in a slow oven (300°F.) for 1¼ hours.

Yield: 8 to 10 servings

Stuffed Cabbage Leaves

10 or 12 large cabbage leaves	¼ teaspoon garlic salt
1 pound ground beef	½ cup chopped onion
2 cups soft ½-inch bread cubes	2 eggs
1½ teaspoons salt	1 can (10½ ounces) condensed tomato soup
¼ teaspoon pepper	

Parboil cabbage leaves for 5 minutes. Combine beef, soft bread cubes, salt, pepper, garlic salt, onion and eggs. Form meat mixture into 10 or 12 oblong patties. Place a meat patty on each of the cabbage leaves. Roll cabbage leaves, and fasten leaves to meat with food picks. Place stuffed cabbage leaves into cold electric skillet. Pour undiluted tomato soup over cabbage rolls. Cover and cook at low heat (260°F.) for 45 minutes.

Yield: 5 to 6 servings (2 cabbage rolls each)

In the 17th century, it was customary for a Bulgarian bridegroom to carry a loaf of fresh bread to the altar to signify that he would provide well for his wife.

Italian Meatballs and Spaghetti

1 pound hamburger
2 teaspoons salt, divided
⅜ teaspoon pepper, divided
1½ cups dry bread crumbs
¼ cup milk
1 tablespoon minced onion
2 tablespoons chopped
parsley
¼ cup margarine
1 can (17 ounces) tomatoes
1 tablespoon butter

1 can (8 ounces)
tomato sauce
2 tablespoons chopped
green pepper
½ cup chopped
mushrooms
1 teaspoon garlic salt
½ pound spaghetti
¼ cup grated
Parmesan cheese

Combine hamburger, 1 teaspoon salt, ¼ teaspoon pepper, dry bread crumbs, milk, onion and parsley. Form into 12 balls. Melt margarine in frypan, then brown meatballs in hot margarine. Combine tomatoes, butter, tomato sauce, green pepper, mushrooms, garlic salt, remaining pepper and salt. Cook slowly in large frypan for 1 hour. Add browned meatballs and cook for an additional 30 minutes. Cook spaghetti according to package directions. Drain. Arrange cooked spaghetti on platter. Pour sauce and meatballs over spaghetti. Top with grated cheese. Yield: 6 large servings (2 meatballs each)

Creamed Dried Beef Deluxe

2 cups milk
2 cans (10½ ounces each)
condensed mushroom
soup
3 packages (4 ounces each)
dried beef

2 cups boiling water
2 tablespoons butter
or margarine
½ cup slivered almonds
6 slices of toast

Combine milk and soup in top part of double boiler. Cook over medium heat, stirring until smooth. Cut dried beef into strips. Add to soup and heat thoroughly. Place top part of double boiler into lower section in

which there are 2 cups of boiling water. Melt butter in 7-inch frypan. Add almonds and brown over medium heat. Serve dried beef mixture over toast. Garnish each serving with browned slivered almonds.
Yield: 6 servings

Party Veal Cutlets

2 pounds veal cutlets, cut ½ inch thick
1 egg, beaten
1 teaspoon salt
¼ teaspoon pepper
1½ teaspoons paprika
⅓ cup dry bread crumbs
3 tablespoons shortening
1 can (4 ounces) mushrooms
½ cup water
1 bouillon cube
1 small garlic clove, minced
1 cup dairy sour cream
2 tablespoons capers

Cut veal into 6 servings. Combine egg, salt, pepper and paprika. Dip veal into egg mixture and then into crumbs. Brown in shortening. Add mushrooms including liquid, water, bouillon cube and garlic. Cover tightly and cook slowly for 45 minutes, or until veal is tender. Remove meat to platter. Add sour cream and capers to liquid in pan. Heat sauce thoroughly and serve over veal.
Yield: 6 servings

Ham Circle Mold

2 tablespoons ham drippings
1 tablespoon flour
1 cup water
2 cups ground cooked ham
1½ cups dry bread crumbs
1 teaspoon onion juice
⅛ teaspoon ground marjoram or sage
⅓ cup diced green pepper
¼ cup chopped celery
1 cup tomato purée
2 eggs, separated

Melt ham drippings in a saucepan. Blend in flour. Add water and cook until thick, stirring constantly. Combine ham, bread crumbs, onion juice, marjoram, green pepper, celery and tomato purée. Add ham gravy. Blend in beaten egg yolks and fold in stiffly beaten egg whites. Place mixture in a greased 1½-quart ring mold. Set mold in a pan of hot water and bake in a moderate oven (350°F.) for 1 hour. Spoon glazed onions into center of ring and serve with horseradish sauce.*

* Horseradish Sauce

¼ cup prepared horseradish
1½ tablespoons vinegar
½ teaspon salt

Dash of cayenne
½ cup heavy cream,
whipped

Combine horseradish, vinegar, salt and cayenne. Add whipped cream. Yield: 8 servings, 1¼ cups sauce

Ham Puff

1 quart toasted ½-inch
bread cubes
1½ cups ground cooked ham
2 tablespoons prepared
mustard
½ teaspoon prepared
horseradish

½ cup fine-chopped celery
4 slices of enriched
bread
4 eggs
2 cups milk
½ teaspoon salt
Dash of pepper

Arrange toasted bread cubes over the bottom of a greased 9-inch-square baking pan. Combine ham, mustard, horseradish and celery. Spread ham mixture over toasted bread cubes. Remove crusts from bread slices and cut diagonally across each slice. Arrange them on top of ham mixture. Beat eggs slightly. Add milk, salt and pepper. Pour liquid mixture over bread and ham, being careful to saturate top slices of bread. Bake in a moderate oven (350°F.) for 45 minutes.
Yield: 6 servings

Cranberry Ham Loaf

2 cups soft coarse
  bread crumbs
3 tablespoons chopped
  fresh parsley
2 tablespoons prepared
  mustard
1 tablespoon instant
  minced onion

1 cup milk
1 egg
1 pound cooked ham,
  ground
½ pound pork
  shoulder, ground
¾ cup whole-
  cranberry sauce

Combine soft bread crumbs, parsley, mustard and onion. Beat milk and egg together. Add to bread-crumb mixture. Thoroughly blend in ground ham and pork. Pack into an ungreased 1-quart loaf pan. Bake in a moderate oven (375°F.) for 1 hour and 15 minutes, or until browned on top. Drain off any excess fat. Invert loaf onto a shallow baking pan or heatproof platter. Spread cranberry sauce over top. Return to oven for about 3 minutes to heat cranberry sauce.
Yield: 6 to 8 servings

Ham Ring with Cherry Sauce

½ cup milk
1½ cups soft rye-bread
  crumbs
1 pound smoked ham,
  ground
1 pound fresh pork, ground

2 tablespoons
  minced onion
2 tablespoons
  minced parsley
1 teaspoon prepared
  mustard
2 eggs, beaten

Pour milk over bread crumbs. Add ham, pork, onion, parsley, mustard and eggs. Mix thoroughly. Pack into a greased 1¼-quart ring mold. Bake in a moderate oven (350°F.) for 1 hour. Serve with cherry sauce (see next page).

Bread made of cornmeal mixed with strawberries was a favorite food of the American Indians.

Cherry Sauce

1 can (16 ounces) pitted
unsweetened red cherries
4 teaspoons cornstarch
¼ cup sugar
⅛ teaspoon salt
⅛ teaspoon ground
cinnamon

⅛ teaspoon grated
nutmeg
Water
Cherry juice
¼ teaspoon red coloring

Drain cherries, reserving juice. Combine cornstarch, sugar, salt, cinnamon and nutmeg. Add enough water to cherry juice to make 1 cup liquid. Add to sugar mixture and stir well. Cook, stirring constantly, until thick and clear. Add cherries and coloring. Cook just until heated through.
Yield: 8 servings

When eating an egg, ladies of the 17th century held the shell daintily and scraped the inside with bread.

POULTRY

Almond and Chicken Casserole

1 package (8 ounces)
  noodles
2 tablespoons butter
2 tablespoons minced
  onion
1 cup thin-sliced celery
2 tablespoons flour
¼ teaspoon dry mustard
2½ teaspoons salt
⅛ teaspoon pepper
2½ cups milk
  2 teaspoons
  Worcestershire sauce

1 cup grated or
  shredded American
  cheese
2 cups diced cooked
  chicken
¼ cup chopped
  pimiento
¼ cup chopped green
  pepper
1 cup roasted almonds,
  chopped, divided
½ cup buttered
  bread crumbs

Cook noodles according to package directions until almost tender. Drain
and rinse with cold water. Melt butter in a saucepan, add onion and

celery, and cook and stir until transparent, about 5 minutes. Blend in flour, mustard, salt and pepper. Add milk and Worcestershire sauce, stirring constantly. Cook until sauce is smooth and thickened. Stir in cheese, chicken, pimiento, green pepper, well-drained noodles and half of the almonds. Turn into a shallow baking dish; sprinkle with crumbs and remaining almonds. Bake in a moderate oven (400°F.) for about 20 minutes, or until thoroughly heated and lightly browned on top.

Yield: 8 to 10 servings

Chicken-Topped Parmesan Toast

1 cup sliced fresh mush-
  rooms, or 1 can (4½
  ounces) mushrooms
	2 cups diced cooked
	  chicken

¼ cup butter	1 teaspoon salt
1 teaspoon minced onion	Dash of white pepper
¼ cup flour	¼ cup small pimiento
2 cups milk	strips
	Parmesan Toast*

Cook mushrooms in butter until tender. Add onion and blend. Add flour and blend. Add milk, stirring constantly, and cook until smooth and thickened. Add chicken, salt and pepper and heat to serving temperature. Fold in pimiento and serve hot on warm Parmesan Toast.*

Parmesan Toast

4 slices of enriched
  white bread
	¼ cup melted butter
	  or margarine
	¼ cup shredded
	  Parmesan cheese

Trim crusts from bread slices. Brush bread with butter. Sprinkle surfaces with cheese. Bake in hot oven (400°F.) until lightly browned, about 7 minutes. Top Parmesan toast with chicken mixture.

Yield: 4 servings

Backyard Chicken

3 broiler-fryer chickens,
  halved or quartered
½ cup butter or margarine
½ cup lemon juice
2 tablespoons soy sauce

½ teaspoon hot
  pepper sauce
2 teaspoons
  barbecue seasoning
2 cups medium-fine
  soft bread crumbs

Wash and dry chicken. Combine butter, lemon juice, soy sauce, hot pepper sauce and barbecue seasoning in small saucepan. Heat until butter is melted. Brush both sides of chicken pieces with sauce. Broil over medium-hot coals for about 15 minutes on each side, brushing with more sauce as chicken is turned. When chicken is lightly browned and almost done, brush again with sauce, roll in bread crumbs, and continue broiling, turning frequently, until chicken is tender and crust is crisp.
Yield: 6 servings

Ham and Almond Creamed Chicken

3 tablespoons butter
  or margarine
3 tablespoons flour
⅛ teaspoon pepper
½ teaspoon salt
1½ cups chicken broth
  or milk

1½ cups chopped
  cooked chicken
1 cup cubed ham
¼ cup sliced
  blanched almonds
8 slices of enriched
  white bread, toasted

Melt butter in a saucepan. Blend in flour, pepper and salt. Add chicken broth and cook until thick, stirring constantly. Add chicken, ham and almonds. Serve hot over 2 slices of toast for each serving.
Yield: 3½ cups

Singapore Chicken Casserole

3 cups ½-inch bread
cubes, toasted
2 cups bean sprouts
⅔ cup sliced water chestnuts
½ cup cut mushrooms
1 teaspoon salt
2 cups diced cooked
chicken

¼ cup sugar
2 tablespoons
cornstarch
¾ cup pineapple juice
¼ cup soy sauce
2 tablespoons vinegar
¼ cup toasted almonds

Combine toasted bread cubes, bean sprouts, water chestnuts, mushrooms, salt and chicken. Combine sugar and cornstarch in a small saucepan. Add pineapple juice and soy sauce. Bring to a boil over medium heat, stirring constantly. Cook for 5 minutes, until thick. Remove from heat and add vinegar. Place chicken mixture in a greased 1½-quart casserole. Pour sauce mixture over chicken and top with toasted almonds. Bake in a moderate oven (350°F.) for 30 minutes. Yield: 6 servings

Cranberry Chicken

3 frying chickens, quartered
6 slices of enriched white
bread, toasted
2 tablespoons chopped
parsley
1 package (8 ounces)
stuffing mix

1 can (10½ ounces) con-
densed chicken-rice soup
½ cup water
2 teaspoons salt
¼ cup melted butter
1 can (1 pound) whole-
cranberry sauce

Wash chicken and pat dry. Cut toast slices diagonally into halves. Combine parsley, stuffing mix, chicken-rice soup and water. Grease a shallow baking pan. Spread out toast triangles in baking pan. Place ⅓ cup stuffing on each piece of toast. Salt chicken pieces and place them, skin side up, over stuffing. Brush butter over chicken. Cover and bake in a hot oven (400°F.) for 30 minutes. Uncover, then bake for 15 minutes. Spread cranberry sauce over chicken. Bake for another 15 minutes. Yield: 12 servings

Malabar Chicken-Salad Puff

2 teaspoons lemon juice
2 teaspoons minced
  crystallized gingerroot
6 tablespoons well-drained
  crushed pineapple
¾ cup chopped cooked
  chicken
¼ cup fine-diced celery

¼ teaspoon salt
2 tablespoons may-
  onnaise or salad
  dressing
2 egg whites
1 cup grated
  American cheese
6 hamburger buns,
  sliced

Add lemon juice and gingerroot to pineapple. Let stand for about 15 minutes. Combine chicken, celery, salt and mayonnaise. Blend in pineapple mixture. Beat egg white until stiff. Fold in cheese. Place ¼ cup of salad mixture on bottom half of each bun. Spread egg-white mixture over salad. Place on baking sheet and bake in a hot oven (450°F.) until browned, about 10 minutes. Toast upper halves of buns to serve as an accompaniment.
Yield: 3 to 6 servings

Chicken Parmesan

2 cups dry bread crumbs
¾ cup grated
  Parmesan cheese
¼ cup chopped parsley
1 teaspoon monosodium
  glutamate
1 teaspoon paprika
1 teaspoon dried orégano

¼ teaspoon dried basil
2 tablespoons salt
⅛ teaspoon pepper
2 broiler-fryer
  chickens, cut into
  serving pieces
1 cup melted butter
  or margarine

Combine dry bread crumbs, cheese, parsley, monosodium glutamate, paprika, orégano, basil, salt and pepper. Dip chicken pieces into melted butter or margarine, then roll in bread-crumb mixture until well coated. Arrange pieces, skin side up, in foil-lined shallow baking pan. Pour remaining butter over chicken. Bake in a moderate oven (350°F.) for

1 hour, or until tender. Baste with pan drippings, but do not turn chicken pieces.

Yield: 8 servings

Hula Chicken

2 broiler-fryer chickens,
cut into serving pieces
2 teaspoons monosodium
glutamate
1½ teaspoons salt
1 egg, slightly beaten
1 can (6 ounces)
frozen pineapple-
juice concentrate,
thawed but undiluted

1⅓ cups fine dry
bread crumbs
¼ cup butter or
margarine, melted
1 can (3½ ounces)
flaked coconut

Rinse chicken pieces. Pat dry with paper towels. Shake monosodium glutamate and salt over both sides of chicken. Combine egg and pineapple concentrate in pie plate. Combine bread crumbs with melted butter in another pie plate. Add coconut and mix well. Coat chicken pieces with pineapple mixture. Then roll in coconut mixture. Place on 2 foil-lined shallow baking pans. Bake in moderate oven (350°F.) for 40 minutes. Reverse pans in oven for even baking. Bake for another 40 minutes. If chicken begins to brown too much before end of baking time, cover loosely with foil; just lay the foil over the chicken but do not cover tightly.

Yield: 8 servings

Criminals of early Hindustan were penalized by being forbidden to eat bread for periods of time, depending on the crime committed. It was believed that to abstain from bread would result in ill health and bad fortune.

Chicken Tetrazzini

¼ cup butter or margarine
½ pound mushrooms, sliced
¼ cup flour
½ teaspoon salt
2 cups chicken broth
1 cup light cream
4 cups diced cooked
    chicken

1 package (8 ounces)
    fine spaghetti,
    cooked
½ cup buttered soft
    bread cubes
¼ cup grated
    Parmesan cheese

Melt butter in saucepan. Add mushrooms and cook over low heat for 5 minutes. Blend flour and salt with mushrooms. Stir in broth and cream. Cook, stirring constantly, until thickened. Combine chicken and spaghetti in a shallow baking dish. Pour sauce over and sprinkle buttered bread cubes and cheese over top. Bake in a moderate oven (375°F.) for 20 minutes, or until brown.

Yield: 8 servings

Chicken Caribé

1 quart soft ½-inch
    bread cubes
¼ cup chopped pimiento
2 tablespoons minced
    parsley
1 teaspoon salt
⅛ teaspoon pepper

3 tablespoons lemon
    juice, divided
2½ tablespoons melted
    butter or margarine,
    divided
2-pound frying
    chicken, quartered

Combine soft bread cubes, pimiento, parsley, salt, pepper, 2 tablespoons lemon juice and 2 tablespoons melted butter. Place a sheet of aluminum foil over a broiler or wire rack set inside a shallow baking pan. Pierce holes in foil with a fork to allow drippings to drain off. Place 4 mounds of stuffing apart from each other on the foil, using 1 cup in each mound. Wash chicken and pat dry. Rub salt on inside of each piece of chicken and place one quarter of chicken over each mound of stuffing. Combine remaining 1 tablespoon of lemon juice and ½ tablespoon melted butter. Brush lemon butter over chicken. Bake in a hot oven (400°F.) for 30 minutes.

Yield: 4 servings

Babe's Chicken à la King

3 tablespoons butter or margarine	1½ cups chicken broth or milk
2 tablespoons minced green pepper	1 can (6 ounces) chopped chicken
⅛ teaspoon pepper	2 tablespoons chopped pimiento
½ teaspoon salt	1 can (2 ounces) button mushrooms
3 tablespoons flour	

Melt butter in saucepan. Add green pepper and sauté for 5 minutes. Blend in pepper, salt and flour. Add chicken broth and cook until thick, stirring constantly. Add chicken, pimiento and mushrooms. Serve hot in Patty Shells.*

*Patty Shells

18 slices of enriched white bread   3 tablespoons melted shortening

Use 3 slices of bread for each patty shell. With a large heart cookie cutter, cut a heart from each slice. With a smaller heart cutter, cut centers from 12 hearts, leaving frames. Stack 2 frames on each large heart base to form a heart patty shell. Brush top, sides and center of each patty shell with shortening. Place shells and heart centers on a greased cookie sheet. Bake in a hot oven (400°F.) for 20 minutes, or until crisp and lightly browned. Serve filled with Chicken à la King. Top each filled patty shell with a heart center.

Yield: 6 servings

In Biblical times, a gift of bread was a token of friendship. To waste bread was an omen of evil, signifying that the guilty person would lose all his friends.

French Toast à la King

8 slices of enriched
white bread
2 eggs, beaten
2⅔ cups milk, divided
⅓ cup margarine
⅓ cup flour
2 cups chopped
cooked chicken

1 can (4 ounces)
chopped mushrooms
½ cup chopped celery
2 tablespoons
chopped pimiento
1 teaspoon salt

Trim crusts from bread and cut each slice diagonally into halves. Combine beaten eggs and ⅔ cup milk. Dip 8 half slices into egg-milk mixture and arrange in the bottom of a 2-quart baking dish. Melt margarine in a 2-quart saucepan. Blend in flour. Add remaining 2 cups of milk and bring mixture to a boil over medium heat, stirring constantly. Remove from heat and add chicken, mushrooms, celery, pimiento and salt. Spoon chicken mixture over bread in bottom of baking dish. Dip remaining 8 half slices of bread into egg-milk mixture and arrange over top of the chicken. Bake in a moderate oven (350°F.) for 30 minutes. Yield: 8 servings

Chicken Patties

⅔ cup shortening, divided
½ cup chopped onion
½ cup chopped celery
4 cups toasted ¼-inch
bread cubes
2 cups diced cooked
chicken
½ cup slivered almonds
½ teaspoon dry mustard

½ teaspoon salt
Dash of pepper
¼ cup water
½ teaspoon
Worcestershire sauce
6 eggs, beaten
1 cup chicken or
mushroom gravy

Melt ¼ cup shortening in a frypan. Add onion and celery and sauté over low heat until tender. Combine toasted bread cubes, chicken, almonds, mustard, salt and pepper. Stir in sautéed onion and celery

with shortening. Combine water and Worcestershire sauce with beaten eggs. Add to bread-cube mixture. Mix well. Form 12 large oval-shaped patties, using ⅓ cup of mixture for each one. Melt unused shortening in skillet or on griddle as needed to fry the patties until golden brown on all sides. Serve with hot chicken or mushroom gravy.
Yield: 6 servings, 2 chicken patties per serving

Chicken and Asparagus Bake

8 slices of enriched
white bread
2 cups chopped
cooked chicken
1 package (10 ounces) cut
asparagus, cooked
1 cup grated
Cheddar cheese

1 can (10½ ounces)
condensed cream of
chicken soup
½ cup milk
¼ cup chopped
pimientos

Trim crusts from bread. Arrange 4 slices on the bottom of an 8-inch-square baking dish. Top with half of the chicken. Arrange cooked asparagus over chicken. Spread remaining chicken over asparagus layer. Top with half of grated cheese. Combine chicken soup, milk and pimientos. Pour half of soup mixture over chicken. Cover with remaining 4 bread slices. Sprinkle with remaining cheese. Pour remaining soup mixture over bread. Bake in a slow oven (325°F.) for 30 minutes.
Yield: 4 servings

A baker's dozen is so widely accepted to be thirteen in South America, there is a monument built with fees collected from bakers who have been arrested for selling less than 13 items in a dozen.

California Supper

3 avocados
Lime juice
3 tablespoons olive oil
or butter
2 tablespoons minced onion
1 garlic clove, minced
3 tablespoons flour
½ teaspoon salt
1 can (8 ounces)
tomato sauce
½ cup chicken broth

1 teaspoon
Worcestershire sauce
⅛ teaspoon hot
pepper sauce
2 cups diced
cooked chicken
¼ cup sliced ripe olives
½ cup grated process
American cheese
1 cup soft bread
crumbs, buttered

Cut avocados lengthwise into halves. Remove pits. Brush cut surfaces with lime juice to prevent discoloration. Set aside. Heat olive oil in frypan. Add onion and garlic. Cook until onion is tender but not brown. Add flour and salt; blend. Combine tomato sauce, broth, Worcestershire sauce and hot pepper sauce. Gradually add to contents of frypan, stirring constantly, until mixture thickens and comes to a boil. Add chicken and olives; heat. Remove from heat, add cheese, and stir until melted. Spoon about ⅓ cup of the hot mixture into the cavity of each avocado half. Top with buttered crumbs. Place in broiler under moderate heat (400°F.). Broil for approximately 4 minutes, or until crumbs are lightly browned. Serve immediately.
Yield: 6 servings

Citrus-Baked Chicken

2 teaspoons grated
lemon rind, divided
1 teaspoon grated
orange rind
½ cup orange juice
2 tablespoons lemon juice
½ cup firmly packed
brown sugar

2 tablespoons sherry
1½ quarts soft ½-inch
bread cubes
⅔ cup chopped parsley
¼ teaspoon salt
1 frying chicken
(3 pounds), quartered

Place 1 teaspoon lemon rind, the orange rind, orange juice, lemon juice and brown sugar into a small saucepan. Bring to a boil and continue simmering for 20 minutes. Remove from heat and add sherry. Combine soft bread cubes, parsley, salt and remaining lemon rind. Place bread mixture in bottom of a lightly greased 9-inch-square baking dish. Top with chicken. Pour half of the sauce over chicken and bake in a moderate oven (350°F.) for 45 minutes. Pour remaining sauce over chicken and cook for an additional 30 minutes.
Yield: 4 servings

Turkey Divan with Cheese Sauce

½ cup butter, divided	2 cups milk
6 thick slices of enriched	1 cup shredded
white bread	American cheese
⅓ cup flour	12 thin slices of
1 teaspoon salt	cooked turkey
½ teaspoon paprika	24 stalks of
Dash of pepper	asparagus, cooked

Melt butter. Cut crusts from bread slices. Brush cut surfaces of bread, using ¼ cup melted butter. Place on an ovenproof platter or baking dish. Place remaining ¼ cup butter in saucepan and blend in flour, salt, paprika and pepper. Add milk, stirring constantly, and cook until sauce is smooth and thickened. Blend in cheese; stir until melted. Toast bread in a very hot oven (450°F.) for about 5 minutes, until lightly browned. Arrange turkey on toast squares. Cover with asparagus tips. Spoon cheese sauce over asparagus. Place under broiler 4 to 5 inches from heat source for 3 to 4 minutes, until heated thorough and lightly browned.
Yield: 6 servings

Every morning in India 300,000,000 Hindus repeat these words from the pages of a prayer book: "Everything is food, but bread is the great mother."

STUFFED & STUFFINGS

To Prepare Stuffing and Roast Poultry

Dress and clean poultry. Melt shortening in a frypan, add onion and celery, and sauté in hot fat for 15 minutes. Combine bread cubes, salt, pepper and poultry seasoning with sautéed mixture. Add water and mix thoroughly. Lightly spoon stuffing into neck cavity, using enough so that poultry will look plump when served. Fold neck skin over and skewer it to back. Fill abdominal cavity with remaining stuffing. Close by sewing the skin together with a heavy string, or by skewering the skin together with metal skewers and lacing with heavy string. Twist wing tips onto back to hold them in place. Tie legs together securely and fasten to tail. Grease skin thoroughly with melted shortening. Place stuffed bird on a rack in roasting pan. Insert a meat thermometer into skin between first and second ribs of turkey so that bulb end rests in the center of the stuffing. Dip a square of cheesecloth into melted fat and cover bird loosely. Roast uncovered in a slow oven (300° to 325°F.) until thermometer registers 165°F. Doneness of meat may also be judged by the ease with which the drumstick can be moved up and down. Also if the thigh meat feels soft when the thickest part is pressed between the fingers, the bird is done.

Allow a 20-minute rest period after removing bird from the oven to assure highest center-of-stuffing temperature and to allow for ease in carving.

Stuffing Pointers

1. To fill lightly the abdominal cavity and neck pocket, allow ¾ cup stuffing per pound of poultry, dressed weight, or 1 cup per pound ready-to-cook weight.
2. Allow the same amount of stuffing for a turkey weighing 20 pounds or more because the abdominal cavities of large birds are approximately the same size as those of smaller birds. The difference in weight is due to the added amount of meat on the carcass.
3. For fluffy light-textured stuffings which are high in flavor, fill the cavity lightly. As the juices are absorbed by the stuffing during the roasting period, stuffing will expand. Overpacking will result in a compact, less desirable foodstuff and may cause the turkey to burst.
4. For safest results, the stuffing should be mixed immediately prior to use. The stuffed bird should be placed in a preheated oven at once. If it is necessary to hold the stuffed poultry before roasting, the stuffing should be chilled before use, and the clean stuffed bird should be refrigerated. The storage time should not be more than 4 hours.
5. Recommended advance preparations for handling stuffing:
   Prepare and measure dry ingredients. Store at room temperature.
   Prepare and measure liquid and perishable ingredients. Refrigerate.
   Combine liquid and dry ingredients at the last minute.
   Fill turkey, truss, and roast immediately.
6. Freezing of prepared stuffings is not recommended. Storing frozen stuffings at 0°F. for 1 week results in wet, uninviting stuffings, and the seasonings take on a bitter flavor.

Poultry Weight (Ready-to-Cook)	4 pounds	6 pounds	10 pounds	12 pounds	20 pounds
STUFFING INGREDIENTS					
Shortening	1/4 cup	1/3 cup	1/2 cup	2/3 cup	1 cup
Chopped onion	1/2 cup	2/3 cup	1 cup	1 1/3 cups	2 cups
Chopped celery	1/2 cup	2/3 cup	1 cup	1 1/3 cups	2 cups
SOFT BREAD CUBES (1/2-inch)	6 cups	9 cups	15 cups	1 1/8 gallons	1 7/8 gallons
OR	or	or	or	or	or
BREAD SLICES (5/8-inch)	6	9	15	18	30
Salt	2/3 teaspoon	1 teaspoon	1 1/2 teaspoons	2 teaspoons	1 tablespoon
Pepper	dash	1/8 teaspoon	1/4 teaspoon	1/4 teaspoon	1/2 teaspoon
Poultry seasoning	1 1/3 teaspoons	2 teaspoons	1 tablespoon	1 1/3 tablespoons	2 tablespoons
Water	1/3 cup	2/3 cup	1 cup	1 1/3 cups	2 cups
Cups of stuffing (average)	4	6	10	12	20

Party Roast Chicken

1 cup butter or margarine	½ teaspoon pepper
½ cup chopped onion	2 teaspoons
1½ cups chopped celery	ground sage
1 gallon soft ½-inch	2 ready-to-cook
bread cubes	roasting chickens or
1 cup buttered roasted	capons (6 pounds
diced almonds	each)
1½ teaspoons salt	⅓ cup melted shortening

Melt butter in a frypan. Add onion and celery and sauté until tender. Pour over soft bread cubes, almonds, salt, pepper and sage. Rinse chickens in cold water and pat dry. Spoon 1 cup stuffing into neck cavities, fold neck skins over, and skewer them to back. Put 5 cups stuffing into body cavity of each chicken. Close body cavity by skewering skin together and lacing it closed. Skewer wings to body until they rest flat against the neck skin. Tie legs together and fasten them to tail. Grease skin with melted shortening. Place stuffed chickens on racks in shallow pans. Insert a meat thermometer through the membrane between the first and second ribs so that bulb end reaches into center of stuffing. Roast uncovered in a slow oven (325°F.) until thermometer reaches 165°F. and chickens are tender.
Yield: 24 servings

Just for Two

1 frying chicken	½ teaspoon salt
(2½ pounds)	1/16 teaspoon pepper
2 tablespoons shortening	1 teaspoon poultry
¼ cup chopped onion	seasoning
½ cup chopped celery	⅓ cup chicken broth
1 quart soft ½-inch	or water
bread cubes	

Buy chicken split down back only. Wash chicken and pat dry with towel. Melt shortening in frypan. Add onion and celery and sauté in

hot fat for 15 minutes. Pour this mixture over soft bread cubes with salt, pepper and poultry seasoning. Add chicken broth and mix thoroughly. Spread chicken apart and fill cavities with the bread stuffing. Fasten chicken halves together with skewers or food picks. Pull neck skin over back and secure with skewers. Lace heavy cord around skewers from neck down center back to tail, and tie. Tie legs together tightly. Brush skin with melted butter or shortening. Place chicken on rack in a baking pan and roast, uncovered, in a moderate oven (350°F.) for 1½ hours. Make gravy with drippings.
Yield: 2 servings

Friday-Night Chicken

½ cup enriched flour
½ teaspoon salt
¼ teaspoon pepper
1 roasting chicken (5 pounds), cut into pieces
⅔ cup shortening, melted
1½ quarts dry bread cubes
¾ teaspoon salt
¼ teaspoon pepper
1 teaspoon poultry seasoning

2 tablespoons minced onion
½ cup fine-chopped celery
½ cup melted butter or margarine
1 can (10½ ounces) condensed chicken broth, divided

Combine flour, salt and pepper in a clean paper bag. Place 1 or 2 chicken pieces at a time into bag and shake until chicken is coated with flour. Remove floured pieces and place in hot shortening in frypan. Fry chicken until golden brown, turning with tongs so it will brown evenly on all sides. Combine bread cubes, salt, pepper, poultry seasoning, onion, celery, melted butter and ½ cup chicken broth. Arrange fried chicken around sides of 3-quart casserole and put stuffing in center. Add enough water to rest of chicken broth to make 2 cups liquid and pour it over chicken. Cover casserole tightly and bake in a moderate oven (350°F.) for 1½ hours, or until chicken is tender. Make gravy with drippings in frypan and serve separately.
Yield: 8 to 10 servings

Roast Cozy Turkey

1½ cups (¾ pound) sausage meat	1 cup chopped celery
1½ quarts toasted bread cubes	¼ cup chopped onion
½ teaspoon salt	¾ cup water
½ teaspoon poultry seasoning	1 ready-to-cook turkey (6 pounds)
	⅓ cup fat

Break sausage into small pieces and place in hot frypan. Brown meat over low heat, turning it as necessary. Pour sausage and drippings over toasted bread cubes with salt, poultry seasoning, celery and onion. Add water and mix thoroughly. Spoon 1 cup stuffing into neck cavity, fold neck skin over, and skewer it to back. Put 3 cups stuffing into body. Close body cavity with skewers and lace with heavy string. Skewer wings to body until they rest flat against the neck skin. Tie legs together and fasten them to tail. Grease skin with fat. Place turkey on rack in baking pan and roast uncovered in a slow oven (325°F.) for 3 hours. Press remaining stuffing into greased muffin pans and bake in oven (325°F.) for last 40 minutes that turkey is roasting. Turn stuffing "muffins" out all at once and arrange them around turkey on platter. Yield: 12 servings

Unbelievable Roast Turkey

1 ready-to-cook turkey (9 pounds)	⅔ cup melted butter or margarine
3 quarts soft ½-inch bread cubes	⅔ cup orange juice
1½ teaspoons salt	Salt
1 teaspoon grated mace	Melted butter or shortening
1½ cups diced mixed glacéed fruits	

Rinse turkey in cold water and pat dry. Refrigerate while stuffing is

prepared. Combine soft bread cubes, salt, mace and fruit mixture. Blend in butter and orange juice. Rub neck and body cavities with salt. Spoon stuffing into neck cavity, using enough to fill the skin so that turkey will look plump when served. Fold neck skin over and skewer it to back. Twist wing tips and fasten them onto back. Put the remaining stuffing into body. Close cavity by skewering skin together and lacing it closed with heavy string. Tie drumsticks to tail. Brush skin thoroughly with melted butter or shortening. Place turkey, breast up, on a rack in a shallow open pan. Insert meat thermometer through the membrane between the first and second ribs, so that bulb end reaches into center of stuffing. Roast uncovered in a preheated slow oven (325°F.) for 3 hours or longer, until stuffing temperature reaches 165°F. Do not sear and do not add water during roasting period.
Yield: 18 servings, 2½ quarts stuffing

McIntosh Turkey

1 frozen turkey roast
(5 to 6 pounds)
1 teaspoon salt, divided
½ teaspoon ground allspice
½ teaspoon ground
cinnamon
1 tablespoon minced onion
½ cup chopped celery

2 cups coarsely
chopped apples
with skins left on
1¼ quarts soft ½-inch
bread cubes
½ cup melted butter
or margarine, divided
1 egg, slightly beaten
¼ cup water
1 teaspoon lemon juice

Thaw turkey roast in refrigerator. Remove any giblets. Wash bird thoroughly; dry. Rub inside with ½ teaspoon salt. Fasten cut edges of skin to meat with skewers. If forequarter is used, cut off the bony tip of wing. Tie or skewer wing to roast. Combine allspice, ½ teaspoon salt, cinnamon, onion, celery and apples with soft bread cubes. Add ¼ cup melted butter. Blend egg with water and lemon juice. Add to bread mixture and toss stuffing lightly with 2 forks. Place a wire rack in a baking pan. Cover with a square of heavy-duty foil. Pierce about

12 small holes in the foil to allow fat to drip through. Fill cavity of roast with stuffing. Mound remaining stuffing, in shape of roast, on the foil. Lay turkey, skin side up, over the stuffing. Brush turkey with part of butter. Roast in a slow oven (325°F.) until tender, about 3 hours. Baste occasionally with remainder of butter or with pan drippings. Serve turkey on a platter. Spoon stuffing into a serving bowl and serve separately.
Yield: 10 to 12 servings

Dindon Châtaigne

1 ready-to-cook turkey
   (6 pounds)
¼ cup butter or margarine
1 cup chopped cooked
   chestnuts or unsalted
   fresh peanuts
½ cup chopped celery

1½ quarts toasted
   bread cubes
⅛ teaspoon pepper
¼ teaspoon grated
   nutmeg
¼ cup water
1 egg, beaten
2 teaspoons salt

Rinse turkey in cold water and pat dry. Refrigerate while stuffing is prepared. Melt butter in a frypan. Add chestnuts and celery and sauté until tender. Combine with toasted bread cubes, pepper, nutmeg, water, beaten egg and 1 teaspoon salt. Rub turkey cavity with 1 teaspoon salt. Lightly fill neck and body cavities of turkey with stuffing. Close body cavity by pushing legs through skin flap near tail of bird. Fasten neck skin to back with skewer. Twist wing tips and fasten tips onto back. Brush skin with melted fat. Place turkey, breast up, on a rack in a shallow pan. Insert a meat thermometer through the membrane between the first and second ribs so that bulb end reaches into center of stuffing. Roast uncovered in a preheated slow oven (325°F.) for 3 to 4 hours, until stuffing temperature reaches 165°F. Do not sear and do not add water during roasting period.
Yield: 12 servings, 1½ quarts stuffing

Because they specialized in selling bread by loaves, bakers of 16th-century England were known as "loafers."

Sweet-Potato Stuffing for Turkey

2 cups mashed sweet
   potatoes
6 cups toasted bread cubes
1 cup chopped celery
2/3 cup chopped onion
8 sausage links

2½ teaspoons salt
½ teaspoon pepper
2 teaspoons poultry
   seasoning
¼ cup butter or
   margarine, melted

Combine sweet potatoes, toasted bread cubes, celery and onion. Cut sausage links into ½-inch pieces, brown, and add to the mixture. Add seasonings and melted butter or margarine. Mix well and spoon lightly into the crop and body cavities of turkey. Close cavities with skewers and lace with heavy string.

Yield: enough stuffing for a 10- to 12-pound turkey

Note: Make half of this recipe to stuff 5- to 6-pound chicken or capon.

Epicurean Delight

1½ quarts soft ½-inch
   bread cubes
¾ teaspoon crushed
   tarragon leaves
¼ cup butter or margarine
½ cup chopped celery

¼ cup chopped onion
1½ cups chopped
   fresh mushrooms
1 chicken bouillon
   cube
⅓ cup boiling water

Toss bread cubes and tarragon leaves together. Melt butter in a large frypan. Add celery, onion and mushrooms. Cook over medium heat until celery, onions and mushrooms are tender, stirring frequently. Dissolve bouillon cube in the boiling water. Combine all ingredients. Used to stuff meat, fish, or poultry.

Yield: 1½ quarts stuffing

Before erasers were known, bread crumbs were used to erase pencil marks.

Coast-to-Coast Stuffing

¼ cup butter or margarine
¼ cup chopped onion
⅓ cup chopped celery
1½ quarts soft ½-inch
   bread cubes
1 teaspoon chopped parsley
1 teaspoon crumbled
   dried sage

3 cups chopped
   cooking apples
⅓ cup raisins, washed
1 chicken bouillon
   cube
¼ cup boiling water

Melt butter in a frypan. Add onion and celery and sauté until tender. Combine soft bread cubes, parsley, sage, apples, and washed raisins. Dissolve bouillon cube in water. Combine all ingredients. Use to stuff meat, fish, or poultry.
Yield: 2 quarts stuffing

Fruit-Stuffed Goose

3 quarts soft bread crumbs
3 cups diced peeled apples
1½ cups seedless raisins,
   washed
1½ cups orange juice

¾ cup sugar
¾ cup melted bacon
   drippings
1 ready-to-cook
   goose (9 pounds)

Combine soft bread crumbs, apples, raisins, orange juice, sugar and bacon drippings. Rinse goose in cold water and pat dry. Spoon stuffing into neck cavity, using enough to fill the skin so goose will look plump when served. Fold neck skin over and skewer it to back. Spoon remaining stuffing into the body. When body is filled, skewer cavity together and lace with heavy string. Skewer wings to body until they rest flat against the neck skin. Cross legs, tie securely with heavy string, and fasten to tail. Place goose on rack in shallow pan. Insert a meat thermometer through the membrane between the first and second ribs, so that bulb end reaches into center of stuffing. Roast uncovered in slow oven (325°F.) until thermometer reaches 165°F.
Yield: 15 to 18 servings, 9 cups stuffing

Turkey with Parsley-Bread Stuffing

1 ready-to-cook turkey
(11 pounds)
½ cup butter or margarine
½ cup chopped onion
1 cup chopped celery
3 quarts dry ½-inch
bread cubes

2 cups chopped parsley
1 teaspoon salt
1 teaspoon dried
thyme
½ teaspoon pepper
2 eggs, beaten
⅓ cup melted shortening

Rinse turkey in cold water and pat dry. Melt butter in a frypan. Add onion and celery and sauté until tender. Pour over dry bread cubes, parsley, salt, thyme and pepper. Add beaten eggs and mix well. Spoon stuffing into neck cavity, using enough to fill the skin so that turkey will look plump when served. Fold neck skin over and skewer it to back. Spoon remaining stuffing into body. When body is filled skewer cavity together and lace with heavy string. Skewer wings to body until they rest flat against the neck skin. Cross legs, tie securely with heavy string, and fasten to tail. Grease skin thoroughly with melted shortening. Place turkey on rack in shallow pan. Insert a meat thermometer through the membrane between first and second ribs, so that the bulb end reaches into center of stuffing. Roast uncovered in a slow oven (325°F.) until thermometer reaches 165°F.
Yield: 20 servings, 11 cups stuffing

Turkey Noisette

⅔ cup butter or margarine
½ cup chopped onion
1 cup chopped celery
3 quarts soft bread crumbs
1 cup chopped
salted peanuts

½ teaspoon salt
½ cup turkey broth
1 ready-to-cook
turkey (5 pounds)
⅓ cup melted shortening

Melt butter in a frypan. Add onion and celery and sauté until tender. Pour over soft bread crumbs, peanuts, salt and turkey broth. Rinse turkey in cold water and pat dry. Spoon 1 cup stuffing into neck cavity. Fold neck skin over and skewer it to back. Put 4 cups stuffing into body. Close body cavity by skewering skin together and lacing it closed. Skewer wings to body until they rest flat against the neck skin. Tie legs together and fasten them to tail. Grease skin with melted shortening. Place turkey on rack in shallow pan. Insert a meat thermometer through the membrane between first and second ribs, so that the bulb end reaches into center of stuffing. Roast uncovered in a slow oven (325°F.) until thermometer reaches 165°F.

Yield: 10 servings

Fresh Cranberry Stuffing

2 cups coarsely chopped
  fresh cranberries
⅓ cup sugar
½ cup chopped celery
¼ cup chopped fresh parsley
½ cup butter or margarine,
  melted
2 quarts toasted
  bread cubes

2 teaspoons salt
¼ teaspoon pepper
1 teaspoon poultry
  seasoning
¼ teaspoon ground
  ginger

Combine cranberries and sugar and let stand for 30 minutes. Sauté celery and parsley in butter or margarine. Add toasted bread cubes, salt, pepper, poultry seasoning and ginger. Mix well. Add cranberries and toss lightly. Spoon into the body and neck cavities. Close openings with skewers and lace with heavy string.

Yield: enough for 10- to 12-pound turkey

Note: For roasting chicken or duck, use ½ recipe.

In Colonial times a loaf of freshly baked bread was sniffed for the relief of head colds.

Celery Stuffing

1 cup chopped onion
2 cups chopped celery
¾ cup butter or margarine,
    melted, divided
2 teaspoons salt

¼ teaspoon pepper
2 teaspoons poultry
    seasoning
2 quarts toasted
    bread cubes

Sauté onion and celery in ½ cup butter until vegetables are limp. Combine with remaining ingredients. Mix well. Spoon lightly into the neck and body cavities of turkey. Close openings with skewers and lace with heavy string.
Yield: enough for 10- to 12-pound turkey
Note: For 5- to 6-pound chicken or capon, use ½ recipe.

Onion and Liver Stuffing

⅔ cup butter or margarine
1 cup chopped fresh onion
½ pound beef liver
½ cup water
1 cup diced celery
2 tablespoons fresh
    parsley

2½ teaspoons salt
2 teaspoons poultry
    seasoning
½ teaspoon pepper
2 quarts toasted
    bread cubes

Melt butter or margarine in large kettle. Add onion and cook until limp. Cook liver in ½ cup water in covered saucepan until tender. Then put through food chopper, using fine blade. Add to butter and onion, along with water in which liver was cooked. Add remaining ingredients. Mix well. Stuff body cavity and neck of turkey. Close openings with skewers and lace with heavy string.
Yield: enough for 10- to 12-pound turkey

In Cairo, Egypt, it is believed that indigestion can be cured by licking the crust of stale bread.

Celery-Nut Stuffing Sticks

1½ quarts ¼-inch bread
  cubes, lightly toasted
⅓ cup chopped nuts
¼ teaspoon poultry
  seasoning

¼ cup water
2 tablespoons butter
  or margarine
1 cup condensed
  cream of celery soup

Combine toasted bread cubes, nuts and poultry seasoning. Add water and butter to undiluted soup and place over low heat until butter is melted, stirring frequently. Toss with bread-cube mixture until blended. Press stuffing into a well-greased 8-inch-square baking pan. Chill for at least 1 hour. Cut into 8 portions and bake in a moderate oven (350°F.) for about 30 minutes, or until lightly browned.

Yield: 8 servings

Raisin-Pineapple Muffins

¼ cup shortening
⅓ cup fine-chopped onion
2 quarts soft raisin-
  bread crumbs

½ teaspoon salt
Dash of pepper
1 can (1 pound, 4
  ounces) pineapple,
  drained

Melt shortening in a frypan. Add onion and sauté until tender. Pour over soft bread crumbs with salt, pepper and pineapple. Mix thoroughly. Press ½ cup bread stuffing into greased muffin pans and bake in a moderate oven (350°F.) for 30 minutes. Turn out "stuffing muffins" all at once and arrange them around meat on serving platter.

Yield: 1 dozen

The Phoenicians of old launched their ships by smashing a disc of native bread against the ship's side, because bread symbolized good luck and long life.

FISH & SHELLFISH

Danish Sandwich Puff

12 slices of day-old bread
6 slices of process
  Cheddar cheese
2 cans (6½ or 7 ounces
  each) tuna in vegetable oil
⅔ cup real mayonnaise
4 eggs
2½ cups milk

½ teaspoon prepared
  mustard
¼ teaspoon hot
  pepper sauce
1 tablespoon minced
  onion
½ teaspoon salt
  Lemon or lime
  slices for garnish

Remove crusts from bread slices. Arrange 6 slices in shallow casserole (8½ x 14 inches). Cover with cheese slices. Blend tuna and mayonnaise in small bowl. Spread tuna mixture on cheese slices. Cover filling with remaining slices of bread. Beat eggs; blend in milk and remaining

ingredients except garnish. Pour over bread. Refrigerate for 1 hour. Bake, uncovered, in a slow oven (325°F.) for about 50 minutes, or until puffy and brown. Garnish with lime or lemon slices. Serve at once.
Yield: 4 to 6 servings

Deviled Tuna Ramekins

⅓ cup butter or margarine
⅓ cup flour
½ teaspoon salt
Few grains of pepper
½ teaspoon chili powder
Few grains of cayenne
1½ cups milk
2 tablespoons
Worcestershire sauce

Dash of hot
pepper sauce
2 cups flaked tuna
1 tablespoon minced
parsley
1½ cups buttered
bread crumbs

Melt butter or margarine. Combine flour, salt, pepper, chili powder and cayenne. Blend with butter. Add milk. Stir over low heat until smooth and thick. Add Worcestershire sauce, hot pepper sauce, tuna and parsley. Spoon into ramekins. Top with buttered crumbs. Bake in hot oven (400°F.) for 10 minutes.
Yield: 6 servings

Tuna Patties

2 cans (7 ounces each) tuna
⅔ cup fine dry bread crumbs
1 small onion, chopped
1 egg

⅔ cup undiluted
evaporated milk
3 tablespoons butter
Creamed Peas*

Drain tuna, saving oil for use in creamed peas. Flake tuna in a medium-size mixing bowl. Add crumbs, onion, egg and evaporated milk, and mix thoroughly. Divide into 12 equal portions and form into patties. Melt butter over low heat in a large frypan. Add tuna patties. Cook over low heat until golden brown, about 5 minutes, then turn and brown other side, about 5 minutes longer. Serve hot with creamed peas.*

* Creamed Peas

1 can (1 pound) peas
2 tablespoons oil from tuna
¼ cup flour

1 cup undiluted
evaporated milk

Empty peas into saucepan and bring to a boil. Stir in oil from tuna. Remove from heat and stir in flour gradually. Add evaporated milk. Cook and stir over low heat until thickened. Serve with Tuna Patties. Yield: 6 servings

Tangy Tuna Casserole

1 package (8 ounces)
elbow macaroni
¼ cup vegetable oil
⅓ cup chopped onion
2 tablespoons flour
⅓ cup chopped green
pepper
1¼ cups milk
½ teaspoon grated
lemon rind

1 tablespoon
lemon juice
1 tablespoon
chopped pimiento
2 cans (7 ounces
each) tuna
⅓ cup buttered
bread crumbs

Cook macaroni according to package directions. Meanwhile place oil in a medium-size saucepan. Add onion and green pepper and cook for about 2 minutes. Blend in flour. Add milk and stir over medium heat until mixture boils and is thick. Add lemon rind and juice and chopped pimiento. In a 2-quart casserole combine macaroni, sauce and tuna. Sprinkle crumbs over the top. Bake in a moderate oven (400°F.) for about 15 minutes, until lightly browned and bubbly.
Yield: 6 to 8 servings

Pan-Fried Shrimps

1 pound raw shrimps
1 teaspoon salt
½ cup flour
1 egg, beaten

½ cup fine dry
   bread crumbs
½ cup margarine
Lemon wedges

Wash shrimps and peel off shells, leaving tails on. Remove dark veins. Rinse in cold water; drain well. Sprinkle lightly with salt. Roll in flour, dip into beaten egg, then roll in bread crumbs. Melt margarine in a heavy frypan over moderately low heat. Arrange shrimps in margarine and fry gently until golden brown on both sides, turning once or twice. Serve at once with lemon wedges.
Yield: 6 servings

Cheddar Salmon Bake

4 ounces medium-size
   noodles
1 can (1 pound) salmon
1 can (10½ ounces)
   condensed tomato soup
1 cup grated
   Cheddar cheese
2 teaspoons lemon juice
1 tablespoon onion
   flakes

1 teaspoon prepared
   mustard
2 teaspoons
   Worcestershire sauce
¾ cup coarse dry
   bread crumbs
2 tablespoons butter
   or margarine

Cook noodles following package directions; drain. Combine liquid drained from salmon, the soup, cheese, lemon juice, onion flakes, mustard and Worcestershire sauce. Mix well. Add noodles and salmon broken into chunks. Mix lightly. Put in a casserole. Mix dry bread crumbs and melted butter and sprinkle over the casserole. Bake in a moderate oven (375°F.) for about 40 minutes.
Yield: 6 servings

In Siam, the native shares his bread or cake with any passerby that asks for a piece. A refusal is rare, since it is a serious breach of etiquette.

Ranch-Style Haddock

1 pound haddock, boned
1 cup water
1 tablespoon butter
or margarine
¾ cup fine-chopped onion
1 garlic clove, mashed
1 medium-size tomato,
diced
1 tablespoon minced
parsley
1 tablespoon minced chives
2 teaspoons salt
Few grains of pepper
Few grains of
grated nutmeg

⅛ teaspoon ground
thyme
⅛ teaspoon ground
tarragon
½ teaspoon
Worcestershire sauce
3 to 4 drops of hot
pepper sauce
3 cups skim milk
4 slices of enriched
white bread, toasted
1 teaspoon grated
lemon rind

Wash fish and cut into serving pieces. Place in a 2-quart saucepan. Add water, cover, and simmer for about 8 minutes, or until fish is tender. Remove fish from broth; reserve broth. Melt butter in a small fry-pan over medium heat. Add onion and garlic and sauté until light brown in color. Combine onion mixture, tomato, parsley, chives, salt, pepper, nutmeg, thyme, tarragon, Worcestershire sauce and hot pepper sauce with fish broth. Cover and simmer for about 25 minutes, or until flavors are well blended. Add skim milk to broth. Return fish pieces to broth and heat to serving temperature, but do not boil. Serve over slices of toasted bread and garnish with lemon.

Yield: 4 servings

The freshness of bread indicated social standing in early Europe. Freshly baked bread was for royalty, one-day old for the nobility, two-day old for the gentry, three-day old for scholars and friars, and four-day old for the peasant.

Elegant Lobster Tails

4 lobster tails (½ pound
  each)
1 quart hot water
¼ teaspoon salt
  Few grains of pepper
1 bay leaf
¼ cup butter or margarine

¾ cup packaged
  bread-stuffing mix
¾ cup coarse dry
  bread crumbs
¼ cup lemon juice
¼ cup milk
⅛ teaspoon paprika

Place frozen tails in a saucepan; add hot water, salt, pepper and bay leaf. Cover pan. Cook lobster tails over low heat for 10 minutes. Drain off hot water and drench tails with cold water. Cut away undershells and remove meat, saving outside shells. Cube lobster meat. Melt butter. Add to stuffing mix and dry bread crumbs. Blend lemon juice and milk into stuffing. Add cubed lobster to stuffing. Stand shells on sides in cooking pan, allowing tails to curl around. Fill each shell with 1 cup stuffing mixture. Sprinkle with paprika. Tie shells with heavy cord. Refrigerate until ready to bake. Bake in a moderate oven (350°F.) for 15 minutes. Remove cords to serve.
Yield: 4 servings

Baked Seafood Newburg

2 cups medium-thick
  cream sauce
1 tablespoon instant
  minced onion
½ teaspoon dry mustard
1 teaspoon parsley flakes
1 teaspoon
  Worcestershire sauce
1 tablespoon lemon juice
3 tablespoons dry sherry
¼ cup pimiento strips

1 can (7 ounces) solid-
  pack tuna
1 can (4½ to 6½
  ounces) shrimps
1 can (5 to 6 ounces)
  crabmeat
⅔ cup coarse dry
  bread crumbs
3 tablespoons butter
  or margarine

Combine cream sauce, seasonings, lemon juice and sherry. Mix well.

Add pimiento, oil from tuna, tuna broken into chunks, and drained shrimps and crabmeat. Mix lightly. Put in a baking dish. Mix bread crumbs and melted butter. Arrange in a border on top of mixture. Bake in a hot oven (425°F.) for about 20 minutes, until heated through.
Yield: 6 servings

Sherried Holiday Oysters

18 slices of enriched
    white bread
¼ cup milk
2 tablespoons melted butter
18 breaded oysters, fried
	1 can (10½ ounces)
	    condensed cream of
	    mushroom soup
	2 tablespoons
	    chopped pimiento
	¼ teaspoon salt
	3 tablespoons sherry

Use 3 slices of bread for each patty shell. Cut each slice into the shape of a star, using a 4-inch star-shaped gelatin mold as a guide. Cut centers from 12 of the stars, using a 1½-inch round cookie cutter. Brush the milk over top side of the solid stars and both sides of the stars with centers cut out. Stack 2 cut-out stars on each solid star to form a patty shell. Brush top, side and center of each patty shell with melted butter. Place shells on a greased cookie sheet. Bake in a hot oven (400°F.) for 10 minutes, or until shells are crisp and lightly browned. Place 3 fried oysters in each patty shell. Heat undiluted mushroom soup, stirring to keep smooth. Add pimiento, salt and sherry. Spoon about 3 tablespoons mushroom sauce over each filled patty shell.
Yield: 6 servings

In rural Italy, the town baker was also the official "letter-writer and reader" for local illiterates, a sideline that helped business.

Oyster Casserole

1 quart toasted ½-inch
  bread cubes
¼ cup chopped onion
½ cup butter or margarine,
  melted, divided
1 pint oysters
¼ teaspoon ground
  sage

1 can (10½ ounces)
  condensed cream
  of celery soup
3 tablespoons lemon
  juice
2 cups fine soft
  bread crumbs
¼ cup chopped
  pimiento

Place toasted bread cubes in a greased 1½-quart baking dish. In a 1-quart saucepan, sauté the onion in half of the melted butter. Drain oysters, reserving ¼ cup of oyster liquor. Stir oyster liquor and sage into condensed soup. Add to onion mixture and heat, stirring to keep smooth. Gradually stir in lemon juice. Add drained oysters to celery sauce. Pour over toasted bread cubes. Combine bread crumbs and pimiento with remaining melted butter. Sprinkle over top of casserole. Bake in a moderate oven (375°F.) for 30 to 35 minutes, or until oysters are cooked and topping well browned.
Yield: 6 servings

Roman Baked Tuna and Beans

2 cans (7 ounces each)
  tuna, drained
2 packages (9 ounces each)
  frozen Italian green beans
½ cup blue cheese dressing

1 cup dairy
  sour cream
2 tablespoons butter,
  melted
2 cups dry
  bread crumbs

Flake tuna into a medium-size bowl. Place frozen green beans in salted water in a large saucepan. Bring water to a boil. Cover, lower heat, and allow to steam for 6 to 8 minutes, or until beans are almost done. Combine beans with tuna. Combine cheese dressing and sour cream. Mix until well blended. Alternate 2 layers each of tuna and beans with dressing mixture in a 1-quart casserole. With a small spatula, make air spaces so that dressing can seep through to the bottom. Combine butter with bread crumbs. Sprinkle them over the top of casserole. Bake in a moderate oven (350°F.) for 15 minutes.

Yield: 8 servings

Coral Bay Scallop

2 cups toasted ½-inch
   bread cubes
1 can (7 ounces) tuna,
   flaked
1 tablespoon lemon juice
3 tablespoons minced
   parsley, divided
½ cup fine-chopped celery
2 tablespoons butter
   or margarine

2 tablespoons flour
½ teaspoon salt
⅛ teaspoon pepper
1 cup milk
½ cup grated
   sharp cheese
2 tablespoons toasted
   sliced almonds

Combine toasted bread cubes, flaked tuna, lemon juice, 2 tablespoons parsley and the celery in a mixing bowl. Melt butter in a small saucepan. Add flour, salt and pepper. Add milk and cook, stirring constantly, until thick. Add cheese and stir until it melts. Combine cheese sauce with first mixture. Pour into a greased 1-quart casserole. Sprinkle almonds over top. Bake in a moderate oven (350°F.) for 25 minutes. Sprinkle remaining chopped parsley over top of baked casserole before serving.

Yield: 6 servings

Among the superstitious peasantry of Europe, it was considered bad luck to have one's child admired too explicitly. The remedy was to toss a slice of fresh-cut bread in the direction of the departing admirer.

Shrimp de Jonghe

1 large garlic clove
1 cup butter or margarine,
   softened to room
   temperature
Pinch of dried tarragon
Pinch of dried marjoram

3 cups fine dry
   bread crumbs
Juice of 1 lemon
3 pounds shrimps,
   cooked and cleaned
Chopped parsley

Mash garlic until it is almost a paste. Add butter, tarragon and marjoram. Cream together until well blended. Add bread crumbs and lemon juice. Blend well. In a buttered baking dish or 6 individual ramekins place alternate layers of shrimps and bread crumb mixture, sprinkling chopped parsley over the top of each layer. Bake in a moderate oven (375°F.) for 20 minutes, or until heated through. Serve immediately.
Yield: 6 to 8 servings

Creole Shrimp Puffs

1 quart soft bread crumbs
1 teaspoon salt
⅛ teaspoon pepper
⅛ teaspoon paprika
3 eggs, beaten
2 cups milk

1½ cups chopped
   cooked shrimps
4 whole cooked
   shrimps
2 tablespoons chopped
   green pepper, divided

Combine soft bread crumbs, salt, pepper, paprika, beaten eggs, milk and chopped shrimps. Put 1 cup shrimp mixture into each of 4 greased individual casseroles. Place a whole shrimp and ½ tablespoon chopped green pepper over top of each casserole. Set casseroles in a pan of warm water. Bake in a hot oven (400°F.) for 30 minutes.
Yield: 4 servings

By custom each servant in a Guatemalan household received, in addition to her wage, five cents a day for sweet bread and one cent a day for rolls.

St. Mary's Dominican Crab Cakes

1 tablespon lemon juice
1 teaspoon prepared
 mustard
2 teaspoons minced onion
2 teaspoons minced
 green pepper
⅛ teaspoon cayenne
¼ teaspoon salt
1 can (10½ ounces)
 condensed cream of
 celery soup

1 hard-cooked
 egg, chopped
2 cups medium-fine
 soft bread crumbs
1 can (7½ ounces)
 crabmeat, flaked
2 tablespoons water
2 eggs, slightly beaten
1½ cups fine dry
 bread crumbs
Fat for frying

Blend lemon juice, mustard, onion, green pepper, cayenne and salt with undiluted soup. Add chopped egg, soft bread crumbs and flaked crabmeat. Divide mixture into 12 portions, using about 3 tablespoons for each. Shape each portion into a flat cake. Refrigerate for 1 hour or longer. Blend water with beaten eggs. Roll chilled crab cakes in dry bread crumbs, then in egg mixture, and again in dry bread crumbs. Fry in hot deep fat (375°F.) for 2 or 3 minutes, or until browned. Drain on absorbent paper and serve hot.
Yield: 6 servings

Deviled Crab on Toast

1 can (7½ ounces)
 crabmeat
2 tablespoons butter
½ cup chopped green
 pepper
⅓ cup chopped onion
2 tablespoons flour
¼ teaspoon dry mustard
⅛ teaspoon paprika
½ teaspoon salt

⅛ teaspoon ground
 marjoram
2½ cups undiluted
 evaporated milk
1 egg, beaten
1 cup shredded process
 American cheese
⅓ cup canned
 tomato paste
6 slices of toast

Drain crabmeat and remove any cartilage. Melt butter in saucepan over low heat. Add green pepper and onion and cook until onion is transparent. Remove from heat. Blend in flour mixed with seasonings. Gradually add evaporated milk, blending thoroughly. Cook over low heat, stirring constantly, until steaming hot and slightly thickened. Remove from heat and add a little of the hot mixture to beaten egg. Stir until well blended, then add egg mixture to first mixture. Stir in cheese and crabmeat. Return to low heat and stir until cheese is melted. Just before serving add tomato paste. Heat to serving temperature and serve immediately on toast.

Yield: 6 servings

Herbed Salmon Scallop

Butter or margarine
Fine dry bread crumbs
1 can (1 pound) red
or pink salmon
1½ teaspoons salt
2 teaspoons marjoram
leaves
1/16 teaspoon pepper

1 cup medium-
thick white sauce
1 cup soft
bread crumbs
3 tablespoons butter
or margarine, melted
Fresh lemon slices
Paprika

Butter 6 individual casseroles. Sprinkle with fine dry bread crumbs. Drain and flake salmon and mix with salt, marjoram and pepper. Turn into crumb-coated casseroles, filling them half full. Spoon white sauce over each. Mix soft bread crumbs with melted butter or margarine. Sprinkle on tops. Bake in a moderate oven (350°F.) for 20 to 25 minutes, or until crumbs are brown. Garnish each with a slice of fresh lemon and a dash of paprika.

Yield: 6 servings

According to an old English belief, one should never borrow or lend bread, for hard times will surely follow the one breaking this rule.

Seattle Salmon Bake

1 cup celery strips
(1 inch x ½ inch)
1 can (1 pound) red salmon,
drained and flaked
1 tablespoon toasted
sesame seeds, if desired
⅔ cup undiluted
evaporated milk,
whipped cold

½ teaspoon salt
3 tablespoons
lemon juice
½ teaspoon pepper
2 cups soft ½-inch
bread cubes
2 tablespoons melted
butter or margarine

Grease a 1½-quart baking dish. Line bottom of dish with celery strips. Combine flaked salmon and sesame seeds. Spread over celery. Combine whipped evaporated milk, salt, lemon juice and pepper. Pour over seasoned salmon. Toss bread cubes with melted butter and arrange them over top of casserole. Bake in a moderate oven (350°F.) for 25 to 30 minutes. Serve hot.
Yield: 6 to 8 servings

Salmon Tetrazzini

1 can (1 pound) salmon
2 tablespoons butter
or margarine
2 tablespoons flour
½ teaspoon salt
Dash of pepper
Dash of grated nutmeg
2 cups salmon liquid
and milk
1 tablespoon sherry

2 cups cooked
spaghetti
1 can (4 ounces) sliced
mushrooms, drained
2 tablespoons grated
Parmesan cheese
2 tablespoons dry
bread crumbs
Watercress

Drain salmon, reserving liquid. Break salmon into large pieces. Melt butter. Blend in flour and seasonings. Add salmon liquid gradually and cook until thick and smooth, stirring constantly. Add sherry. Mix half of the sauce with the spaghetti and mushrooms. Place in a well-greased

2-quart casserole. Mix remaining sauce with salmon. Place in center of spaghetti. Combine cheese and crumbs. Sprinkle over top of salmon mixture. Bake in a moderate oven (350°F.) for 25 to 30 minutes. Garnish with watercress.

Yield: 6 servings

Salmonburgers

1 can (1 pound) salmon	1 teaspoon dry
½ cup chopped onion	mustard
¼ cup butter or other	½ teaspoon salt
fat, melted	½ cup dry bread
⅓ cup dry bread crumbs	crumbs
2 eggs, beaten	Fat for frying
¼ cup chopped parsley	6 buttered round buns
	Lemon wedges

Drain salmon, reserving ⅓ cup liquid. Flake salmon. Cook onion in butter until tender. Add reserved salmon liquid, crumbs, eggs, parsley, mustard, salt and salmon. Mix well. Shape into 6 cakes and roll in crumbs. Place cakes in a heavy frypan which contains about ⅛ inch of fat, hot but not smoking. Fry at moderate heat. When cakes are brown on one side, turn carefully and brown on the other side; cooking time, 5 to 8 minutes. Drain on absorbent paper. Place cakes in buns. Serve with lemon wedges.

Yield: 6 servings

London's Bread Street was the name of the thoroughfare where the old bread market was located.

Creole Stuffed Salmon

1½ tablespoons melted butter
  or margarine
⅓ cup chopped celery
3 tablespoons chopped
  green pepper
2½ cups soft ½-inch
  bread cubes
3 tablespoons chopped
  stuffed olives

⅛ teaspoon pepper
¼ teaspoon paprika
1 tablespoon lemon
  juice
3 tablespoons
  hot water
4 salmon steaks,
  ½ inch thick

Melt butter in frypan. Add celery and green pepper. Sauté until tender.
Pour over soft bread cubes, olives, pepper and paprika. Add lemon
juice and water. Mix well. Arrange steaks in a greased baking pan.
Place ½ cup stuffing in each of the openings formed by the ends of
the steaks. Bake in a moderate oven (400°F.) for 30 minutes.
Yield: 4 servings

Clam-Stuffed Fish Fillets

2 packages (1 pound each)
  fish fillets
2 cans (5 ounces each)
  minced clams
½ cup butter or margarine
¼ cup chopped onion

¼ cup chopped celery
4 cups soft bread
  crumbs
2 tablespoons
  lemon juice
Salt and pepper

Let fish fillets thaw on refrigerator shelf or at room temperature. Arrange half of fillets, close together, in buttered baking dish. Drain
minced clams, reserving liquid. Melt butter or margarine in frypan. Pour
off about half of butter and reserve. To butter remaining in frypan add
onion and celery and cook until tender. Stir in bread crumbs until butter
is soaked up. Continue tossing crumbs until they brown slightly. Stir
in clams, lemon juice, and enough clam liquid to moisten. Season with
salt and pepper to taste. Spoon stuffing over fillets. Cover with remaining fillets. Brush with reserved butter. Bake in a moderate oven (375°F.)

for 20 minutes, or until fish flakes easily when tested with a fork. Serve in baking dish.
Yield: 6 to 8 servings

Sole Française

2 pounds fillets of sole	Dash of pepper
1 egg yolk	1½ cups fine dry
½ cup milk	bread crumbs
Pinch of salt	Peanut oil

Cut fillets of sole diagonally into ½-inch strips. Blend egg yolk, milk, salt and pepper. Soak fish strips in mixture for a few minutes. Coat fish with bread crumbs, then roll each piece between palms to get a rounded strip. Fry in hot oil (370°F.) until golden brown, about 3 minutes.
Yield: 4 servings

Baked Fish Caribbean

2 tablespoons butter or margarine, melted	3 cups soft ¼-inch bread cubes, toasted
⅓ cup chopped onion	2 tablespoons chopped pimiento
2 tablespoons chopped green pepper	3 tablespoons hot water
½ teaspoon celery salt	Salt
Dash of pepper	2 pounds frozen fish fillets, thawed
¼ teaspoon ground thyme	
¼ teaspoon dry mustard	

Combine melted butter, onion and green pepper in small frypan. Sauté until onion is just tender. Mix celery salt, pepper, thyme and mustard with toasted bread cubes. Blend in sautéed vegetables, pimiento and hot water. Lightly salt the fillets. Spread about ⅓ cup stuffing mixture on each fillet and roll up from narrow end. Wrap each rolled fillet in a strip of foil that is only slightly wider than the fillet, making a double fold where the two ends meet. Turn back edges so stuffing is exposed on both ends of roll. Stand wrapped fillets on ends in a greased baking dish. Bake in a moderate oven (350°F.) for 30 minutes, or until fish is tender. Unwrap and serve with Parsley-Lemon Butter.*

Parsley-Lemon Butter

½ cup butter or margarine, melted
2 tablespoons lemon juice

3 tablespoons minced fresh parsley

Combine melted butter, lemon juice and minced parsley. Heat and serve over stuffed fish fillets.
Yield: 6 to 8 servings

Almond-Topped Fish

1 teaspoon lemon juice
2 tablespoons creamy French dressing
1 package (1 pound) frozen haddock or sole fillets, thawed

1½ cups seasoned bread-stuffing mix
2 tablespoons slivered almonds
2 tablespoons butter or margarine, melted

Combine lemon juice and French dressing. Brush over both sides of fish fillets. Crush bread-stuffing mix with a rolling pin. Dip fish fillets into stuffing mix, turning to coat both sides. Place coated fish flat in a well-greased baking dish. Sprinkle almonds over fish. Drizzle melted butter over top. Bake in a moderate oven (350°F.) for 25 to 30 minutes, or until browned.
Yield: 4 to 5 servings

In Morocco, most families knead their own bread and send the round flat cakes to the public oven, where a certain proportion is retained for payment. The same custom prevails in many rural parts of Europe.

Pike Bake

½ cup tomato sauce
3 tablespoons chopped
onion
2 tablespoons melted
shortening
1 tablespoon chopped
green pepper
½ teaspoon celery salt
¼ teaspoon poultry
seasoning

⅛ teaspoon pepper
1 quart soft ½-inch
bread cubes
1 pike (1½ pounds),
cleaned
1 tablespoon melted
butter or margarine
⅛ teaspoon paprika

Combine tomato sauce, onion, shortening, green pepper, celery salt, poultry seasoning and pepper. Simmer over low heat for 5 minutes. Add to bread cubes and mix thoroughly. Place ½ cup stuffing lightly in cavity of cleaned pike and skewer sides together. Combine melted butter and paprika and carefully brush it over pike. Place in a greased baking pan. Shape remaining stuffing into 6 balls, using ¼ cup per ball, and place in same pan with pike. Bake in hot oven (400°F.) for 20 minutes. Remove skewers and serve on a hot platter, plain or with a sauce.
Yield: 3 servings

Cheese-and-Bread-Stuffed Perch

¼ cup shortening
2 tablespoons chopped
onion
½ teaspoon salt
⅛ teaspoon pepper
3 cups soft ½-inch
bread cubes

½ cup grated sharp
cheese
¼ cup water
4 perch fillets

Melt shortening in frypan. Add onion and sauté until tender. Combine with salt, pepper, bread cubes, cheese and water. Place ½ cup stuffing on skin side of each perch fillet. Roll up fillet from narrow end, with skin side turned in. Place in a greased baking pan, arranging fillets so overlapping edges are down. Bake in a hot oven (400°F.) for 30 minutes. Serve with tartar sauce.

Yield: 4 servings

Tuna-Mushroom Casserole

4 ounces thin egg noodles
4 tablespoons corn oil,
  divided
1 tablespoon minced onion
1 envelope (2½ ounces)
  cream of mushroom soup
  mix
2 cups water
1 cup milk

1 can (7 ounces) tuna,
  drained and flaked
1 garlic clove, sliced
  thin
½ cup fine dry bread
  crumbs
2 tablespoons chopped
  parsley

Cook noodles according to package directions. Drain. Heat 2 tablespoons corn oil in saucepan. Add onion. Cook over low heat, stirring frequently, until tender. Gradually stir in soup mix and water. Bring to a boil, stirring constantly. Remove from heat. Mix in milk and tuna. Combine with cooked noodles. Turn into well-greased 1½-quart casserole. Cook garlic in remaining 2 tablespoons corn oil in frypan over medium heat until lightly browned. Remove garlic. Add bread crumbs to oil; toss lightly. Stir in parsley. Sprinkle over casserole. Bake in a moderate oven (375°F.) until thoroughly heated, about 30 minutes.

Yield: 6 servings

Bread baked on Good Friday was retained far into the year in early times since it was regarded as an excellent precaution against one's house catching on fire.

Tuna Fondue

1 large onion, sliced
¼ cup butter, divided
12 slices (½-inch thick)
  Vienna bread or enriched
  white bread
3 eggs
3 cups milk
1 tablespoon prepared
  mustard
1 teaspoon Worcestershire
  sauce

1 teaspoon salt
1 can (12 ounces)
  tuna, drained and
  flaked
2 cups shredded
  Swiss cheese
¼ cup grated
  Parmesan cheese
Paprika

Slice onion, separate into rings, and sauté in butter until soft. Spread one side of bread slices with a small amount of butter. Beat eggs slightly, add milk, mustard, Worcestershire sauce and salt, and blend. Place 4 slices of bread in a single layer in a buttered 1½-quart casserole, trimming crusts if necessary. Top with layers of one third of onion rings and melted butter, one third tuna and one third Swiss cheese. Repeat to make 2 more layers. Pour egg mixture over top. Top with Parmesan cheese and paprika. Cover. Chill for at least 1 hour, or overnight if possible. Thorough chilling makes the fondue light and puffy. Bake, uncovered, in a moderate oven (350°F.) for 45 minutes, or until puffed and golden. Serve at once.
Yield: 6 to 8 servings

Natives of Sicily regard it as sacreligious to eat bread with their hats on.

Mexican Tuna and Corn Casserole

2 cans (7 ounces each) tuna
1 package (10 ounces)
  frozen whole-kernel corn
  with peppers in butter
  sauce
¼ cup chopped onion
3 tablespoons butter or
  margarine

¼ cup enriched flour
2 cups milk
1 egg, beaten
½ teaspoon salt
¼ teaspoon pepper
¼ teaspoon paprika
1 quart soft ½-inch
  bread cubes

Drain tuna. Break into small pieces. Cook corn according to package directions. Sauté onion in butter. Add flour. Gradually add milk, stirring constantly. Add beaten egg, salt, pepper and paprika. Cook until slightly thickened. Fold in corn, tuna and soft bread cubes. Pour into a greased 1½-quart casserole and bake in moderate oven (350°F.) for 1 hour.

Yield: 6 to 8 servings

Summer Delight

¼ cup butter or margarine
1½ tablespoons lemon juice
1 quart soft ½-inch bread
  cubes
2 cups bite-size pieces of
  head lettuce
1 tablespoon thin-sliced
  green onion
2 tablespoons
  chopped green
  pepper

¼ cup sliced radishes
¾ teaspoon salt
⅛ teaspoon pepper
1 can (7 ounces)
  white tuna, drained
  and broken into
  chunks
3 tablespoons creamy
  slaw dressing

Melt butter in large frypan. Blend in lemon juice. Add soft bread cubes, then brown them in the lemon butter over low heat, turning them often as they toast. Cool. Combine lettuce pieces, green onion, green pepper, radishes, salt, pepper and tuna chunks. Stir in salad dressing. Refrigerate

salad. At serving time, stir in croutons, then immediately serve in salad bowls. A tomato wedge may be used as garnish, if desired.
Yield: 6 servings

Dib's Tuna Bake

2 cups seasoned bread-
    crouton stuffing mix
1 can (1 pound) tomatoes
1 can (7 ounces) tuna,
    drained and flaked
2 thin slices of onion,
    broken into rings
2 thin slices of green
    pepper, cut into
    1-inch strips

4 stuffed olives,
    sliced thin
1 can (10¾ ounces)
    condensed
    Cheddar-cheese
    soup
½ cup soft bread crumbs
1 tablespoon butter,
    melted

Place seasoned croutons in a greased 1½-quart casserole. Drain tomatoes, reserving juice, and slice the tomatoes. Top croutons with about two thirds of the sliced tomatoes and the flaked tuna, onion rings, green-pepper strips and sliced olives. Blend ⅓ cup juice drained from tomatoes with undiluted cheese soup. Pour over ingredients in casserole. Top cheese sauce with remaining tomato slices. Toss bread crumbs with melted butter. Scatter over top of casserole. Bake in a moderate oven (375°F.) for 40 minutes, or until mixture is hot and crumbs are browned.
Yield: 6 servings

In Morocco, stale bread is considered excellent for curing stuttering.

EGGS & CHEESE

Puccini Bake

3 eggs, separated
1 cup dairy sour cream
1 cup small-curd cottage cheese
1 tablespoon instant minced onion
⅛ teaspoon instant garlic granules
2 tablespoons chopped chives

1½ teaspoons Worcestershire sauce
2 tablespoons toasted sesame seeds
½ teaspoon salt
2½ cups toasted ½-inch bread cubes
⅓ cup Parmesan cheese

Beat egg yolks well. Add sour cream, cottage cheese, onion, garlic, chives, Worcestershire sauce, sesame seeds and salt. Beat egg whites until stiff but not dry. Fold toasted bread cubes and egg whites into first mixture. Pour into a greased 1½-quart baking dish. Bake in a slow oven

(325°F.) for 1 hour. Remove from oven and sprinkle with Parmesan cheese. Serve immediately.

Yield: 6 servings

Danish Cheese Soufflé

2 cups milk
2 tablespoons grated onion
3 cups soft ½-inch bread
  cubes, divided
  Dash of hot pepper sauce
½ teaspoon dry mustard
  Salt and pepper

3 cups grated sharp
  Cheddar cheese
4 eggs, separated
1 tablespoon melted
  butter
1 teaspoon poppy
  seeds

Combine milk and onion in saucepan. Heat to scalding. Add 2 cups bread cubes, hot pepper sauce, mustard, salt and pepper to taste and cheese. Stir until melted. Beat egg yolks slightly. Stir in a little of cheese mixture. Stir into remaining cheese mixture. Cool slightly. Beat egg whites stiff. Fold in. Turn into 1½-quart casserole. Toss remaining bread cubes with melted butter and poppy seeds. Scatter over top of casserole. Bake in moderate oven (350°F.) for 45 to 50 minutes.

Yield: 4 servings

Cheddar Chiffon

2 cups fine soft bread
  crumbs
1 cup milk
½ teaspoon salt
⅛ teaspoon paprika

½ pound sharp
  Cheddar cheese,
  grated
4 eggs, separated

Combine soft bread crumbs, milk, salt, paprika and cheese in a 1-quart saucepan. Place over low heat and cook until cheese melts, stirring constantly. Remove from heat and let stand while preparing other ingredients. Beat egg whites until stiff. Beat egg yolks until thick.

Gradually add bread mixture to beaten egg yolks, continuing to beat until mixture is smooth. Slowly pour egg-yolk mixture over egg whites. At the same time, gently but thoroughly fold the 2 mixtures together. Pour into an ungreased 1½-quart soufflé dish or straight-sided baking dish. To form a crown: Use a teaspoon and make a 1-inch shallow path in the mixture, about 1 inch in from edge of dish. Bake in a slow oven (300°F.) for 1 hour and 15 minutes. Serve at once.
Yield: 4 servings

Mushroom-Topped Rabbit

2 tablespoons butter or
   margarine, divided
2 tablespoons flour
⅓ teaspoon salt
   Dash of cayenne
¼ teaspoon dry mustard
½ teaspoon
   Worcestershire sauce

1 cup milk
1½ cups grated
   American cheese
1 cup sliced fresh
   mushrooms
6 slices of enriched
   white bread, toasted

Melt 1 tablespoon butter in top part of double boiler. Blend in flour, salt, cayenne, mustard and Worcestershire sauce. Add milk and cook, stirring constantly, until thick. Add cheese and stir until it melts. Melt remaining tablespoon butter in frypan. Add mushrooms and sauté for 5 minutes. Pour hot cheese sauce over 1 slice of toast, cover with second slice and pour more sauce over it. Arrange sautéed mushrooms over top of each serving.
Yield: 3 servings

The very first bread was made of acorns, during the Stone Age, more than 240,000 years ago.

Cheddar Cheese Casserole

6 slices of enriched white
  bread, cut into ½-inch
  cubes
½ pound Cheddar-cheese
  slices
3 eggs

½ teaspoon salt
½ teaspoon paprika
¼ teaspoon dry mustard
2½ cups milk
  Pinch of cayenne

In a buttered 1½- to 2-quart casserole arrange alternate layers of bread and cheese, ending with cheese. Beat eggs, add rest of ingredients to the eggs, and pour over cheese. Bake, uncovered, in a moderate oven (350°F.) for approximately 1 hour. Serve hot.
Yield: 6 to 8 servings

Swiss Fondue

1 pound Swiss cheese,
  shredded
3 tablespoons cornstarch
½ teaspoon salt
¼ teaspoon white pepper
¼ teaspoon freshly
  grated nutmeg

2 cups buttermilk
1 garlic clove
1 loaf of enriched
  white bread

Toss Swiss cheese with cornstarch, salt, white pepper and nutmeg. Heat buttermilk with garlic clove in a saucepan or chafing dish over low heat. When hot, remove garlic and add Swiss cheese. Stir constantly until cheese is melted. Serve from a chafing dish. Toast slices of bread and cut each into quarters. Each person serves himself from the common dish of fondue, dunking a chunk of toast speared on a long fork into the fondue.
Yield: 6 servings

The bread ration of the Continental private was fixed at one pound per day. Since the Revolution approximately one pound of bread has always formed part of the American soldier's daily ration.

Dairy Treat

8 slices of enriched white
bread
3 tablespoons butter or
margarine, melted
8 slices of bacon

½ cup grated sharp cheese
8 eggs
1 cup dairy sour cream
2 tablespoons chopped
. parsley

Brush butter on both sides of each bread slice and trim crusts. Gently press each slice of bread down into a custard cup to form a bread cup. Cut bacon slices into halves, fry, and drain. Place 2 half slices of bacon in each bread cup, allowing ends to extend over bread. Spoon grated cheese over bacon. Beat eggs and blend in sour cream and parsley. Pour egg mixture into custard cups. Bake in a moderate oven (350°F.) for 25 minutes. Let stand for 1 or 2 minutes before removing from custard cups to serve.

Yield: 8 servings

Quebec Special

8 slices of enriched white
bread
2 teaspoons butter or
margarine
4 eggs
1 teaspoon Worcestershire
sauce

1 can (11 ounces)
condensed cheese
soup
½ cup milk
2 tablespoons minced
green pepper

Trim crusts from bread slices. Butter 4 slices. Place 4 slices, buttered sides down, in a greased 8-inch-square baking dish. Make an indentation in the center of each. Break an egg over each slice. Cut a 1½-inch circle from center of remaining 4 slices. Place over eggs so that yolk is in center hole. Combine Worcestershire sauce, undiluted soup, milk and green pepper. Pour evenly over and around egg sandwiches. Bake in moderate oven (350°F.) for 20 minutes, or until eggs are set.

Yield: 4 servings

Mama's Special

1 pound sausage meat	½ cup orange juice
1 cup mashed potatoes	2 tablespoons butter
6 slices of enriched white	or margarine
bread	Grated rind and
6 eggs	sections of 2 oranges
¾ teaspoon salt	6 parsley sprigs

Cook sausage, breaking up meat and browning well. Drain. Combine cooked sausage with mashed potatoes. Toast bread in a shallow baking pan on one side. Spread sausage-potato mixture over toasted sides and brown under medium broiler heat. Beat eggs slightly. Add salt and orange juice. Beat until blended. Cook slowly in buttered frypan. Divide eggs into 6 portions. Arrange over potato mixture. Garnish each serving with 2 or 3 orange sections, some grated rind, and a sprig of parsley. Yield: 6 servings

Pride of Holland

⅓ cup diced raw bacon	¼ cup milk
2 cups soft ½-inch bread	¼ teaspoon salt
cubes	Dash of pepper
6 eggs	

Place bacon in frypan and start it frying. When bacon fat accumulates in frypan, add soft bread cubes. Continue frying until bacon is crisp and bread cubes are browned. Combine and beat eggs, milk, salt and pepper together slightly. Pour egg mixture over bacon and bread. Cook slowly, stirring occasionally, and scraping the egg from the bottom and sides of pan. Do not overcook. Yield: 6 servings

White bread (called manchet) was baked for and eaten only by nobles in Medieval England; lower classes ate black bread, tradesmen, brown bread.

Top of the Morning

6 slices of enriched white
   bread
2 tablespoons melted
   butter or margarine
6 eggs, beaten

¼ cup milk
1 teaspoon salt
¼ cup grated sharp
   process cheese

Remove crusts from bread. Brush both sides of each bread slice with butter. Gently press each slice into a large custard cup. Combine beaten eggs, milk, salt and cheese. Pour ⅓ cup of egg mixture into each bread cup. Place custard cups in a rimmed shallow pan and bake in a moderate oven (350°F.) for 30 minutes. Serve with sausage.
Yield: 6 servings

Deviled-Egg Casserole

6 hard-cooked eggs
1 tablespoon chopped
   parsley
1 teaspoon minced onion
1¾ teaspoons salt, divided
⅓ cup mayonnaise or salad
   dressing
⅓ cup shortening
⅓ cup sifted all-purpose
   flour

Dash of pepper
2 cups milk
½ pound Cheddar
   cheese, grated
8 ounces egg noodles,
   cooked and drained
1 cup soft bread
   crumbs

Cut eggs lengthwise into halves. Remove yolks, mash, and combine with parsley, onion, ¼ teaspoon salt and mayonnaise. Fill whites. Set aside. Melt shortening in saucepan and stir in flour, remaining 1½ teaspoons salt and pepper. Add milk gradually. Cook and stir over low heat until sauce comes to a boil. Add cheese and stir until melted. Combine half of cheese sauce with cooked noodles. Place in greased baking dish (12 x 8 x 2 inches) and arrange stuffed eggs on top. Cover with remaining sauce and sprinkle top with bread crumbs. Bake in moderate oven (350°F.) for 20 to 25 minutes, or until crumbs are brown.
Yield: 6 servings

Avocado American Treat

2 tablespons soft butter or
  margarine
8 slices of enriched white
  bread
3 tablespoons mayonnaise
  or salad dressing
4 slices of American
  cheese

¼ cup pickle relish
1 avocado, peeled and
  sliced
2 teaspoons fresh
  lemon juice
Salt

Butter bread slices on one side. Spread each buttered slice with mayonnaise. On each of 4 slices of bread, place 1 slice of American cheese, 1 tablespoon pickle relish and one fourth of avocado slices. Drizzle a little lemon juice and sprinkle a little salt over the avocado slices. Top avocado with another slice of bread.
Yield: 2 to 4 servings

Dad's Hearty Rabbit

2 cups buttered cooked rice
1 medium-size onion,
  chopped
½ medium-size green
  pepper, chopped
2 tablespoons butter or
  margarine
1 can (12 to 16
  ounces) whole-kernel
  corn

1 can (1 pound) tomatoes
2 slices of enriched
  white bread, cut into
  ½-inch cubes
¼ teaspoon salt
1 teaspoon
  Worcestershire sauce
1 egg
2 cups grated sharp
  Cheddar cheese

Spread rice in bottom of a shallow casserole. Cook chopped onion and green pepper in butter in frypan until tender. Add drained corn, tomatoes, bread cubes and seasonings. Mix. Stir in beaten egg and cheese. Pour over rice. Bake in a moderate oven (375°F.) for about 30 minutes.
Yield: 6 servings

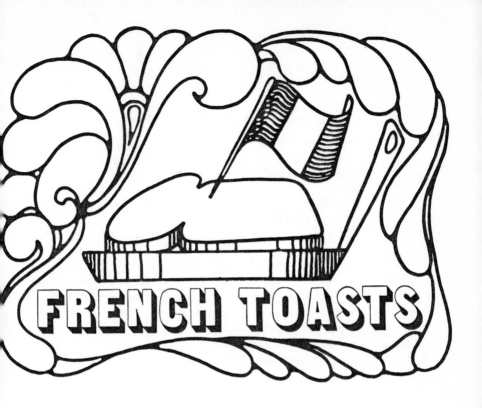

FRENCH TOASTS

French Toast

2 eggs, slightly beaten
⅔ cup milk
¼ teaspoon salt
8 slices of enriched
white bread

¼ cup butter or
margarine
Cinnamon sugar

Combine eggs, milk and salt. Dip bread slices into egg mixture, turning to coat both sides. Brown bread on both sides in small amount of hot butter in a skillet. Sprinkle with cinnamon sugar.
Yield: 4 servings, 2 slices each

California French Toast

2 eggs, slightly beaten
½ teaspoon salt
2 tablespoons granulated
  sugar
1 cup milk
½ teaspoon almond
  extract

12 slices of enriched
  white bread
2 tablespoons
  confectioners' sugar
Slivered almonds

Combine beaten eggs, salt, granulated sugar, milk and almond extract in a shallow dish. Dip bread into egg mixture, 1 slice at a time, turning slices to coat both sides. Place dipped slices on a well-greased cookie sheet. Brown in a hot oven (450°F.) for 7 minutes. Turn toast and continue browning. Sift confectioners' sugar and slivered almonds over top of each slice. Serve immediately.
Yield: 6 servings, 2 slices each

Mother's French Fried Toast

1 egg, slightly beaten
½ cup milk
¼ cup flour
¼ teaspoon salt

¼ teaspoon double-
  acting baking powder
6 slices of enriched
  white bread
Fat for frying

Combine beaten egg, milk, flour, salt and baking powder in a shallow bowl. Dip each slice of bread into egg mixture, turning to coat both sides. French fry toast in deep fat heated to 375°F. on a frying thermometer. Use frying basket to submerge bread until golden brown.
Yield: 3 servings, 2 slices each

To ward off rheumatism, Edgar Allan Poe always carried a slice of bread in one pocket and a cookie in another—an old superstition.

Squash and Oyster Bake

4 small acorn squash
⅓ cup melted butter or
    margarine, divided
2 tablespoons minced
    onion
½ cup fine-chopped celery
1½ cups small oysters, or
    2 cans (12 ounces each)
    small oysters, drained
½ teaspoon salt

⅛ teaspoon pepper
½ teaspoon
    Worcestershire sauce
¾ cup creamy French
    dressing
1 quart soft ½-inch
    bread cubes
1 cup grated Cheddar
    cheese

Clean squash. Cut crosswise into halves. Remove seeds and stringy portions. Brush 2 tablespoons butter over the bottom of an oblong 2-quart baking dish. Place squash, cut sides down, into butter. Cover and bake in a moderate oven (350°F.) for 30 minutes. Remove from oven, uncover, and turn squash over. Sauté onion, celery and oysters in remaining butter until tender. Add salt, pepper, Worcestershire sauce, French dressing and soft bread cubes. Place ½ cup stuffing in each squash half. Top with grated cheese. Bake in a moderate oven (350°F.) for 30 minutes.

Yield: 8 servings

Garden Treat

½ cup butter or margarine,
  divided
3 firm ripe tomatoes
3 eggs

1½ cups fine dry bread
  crumbs
½ teaspoon salt

Melt ¼ cup butter in large frypan. Leave skins on tomatoes, wash, then remove cores at top and slice each one into 4 equal-sized slices. Beat eggs in a small bowl. Put bread crumbs in a shallow pie plate. Sprinkle salt over tomatoes. Coat each tomato slice with crumbs, then with egg, and again with crumbs. Pan-fry breaded tomato slices in butter on both sides. Add remaining butter as needed to fry rest of tomato slices. Serve hot.

Yield: 6 servings, 2 slices each

William's Caesar Salad

2 garlic cloves
¼ cup olive oil
2½ cups soft ½-inch bread
  cubes
2 heads of chilled romaine,
  escarole, or leaf lettuce
½ teaspoon salt
¼ teaspoon pepper

¼ cup grated Parmesan
  cheese
2 tablespoons
  crumbled Danish
  Blue cheese
1 egg, slightly beaten
2 tablespoons lemon juice

Cut garlic cloves into quarters and soak pieces in olive oil for at least 2 hours before using. Put 2 tablespoons garlic oil in frypan, add bread

cubes, and brown them, turning constantly. Tear romaine into medium-size pieces and put them in a large mixing bowl. Sprinkle salt, pepper, Parmesan cheese and blue cheese over romaine. Drizzle rest of garlic oil over all. Drop slightly beaten egg and lemon juice over ingredients. Toss salad gently. Just before serving, add croutons and toss salad again to mix croutons into salad without making them soggy. Anchovy fillets or crisp bacon pieces may be added to salad.
Yield: 6 to 8 servings

Romano Green Beans

2 packages (9 ounces each) frozen cut green beans
1 tablespoon salt
¼ teaspoon grated mace
10 slices of onion
1 tablespoon olive oil

¼ cup butter or margarine
1 cup ¼-inch bread cubes, toasted
½ cup fine-grated Romano cheese

Cook beans according to package directions, adding salt, mace and onion slices to the boiling water. Drain. Stir olive oil and butter into hot beans until butter is melted. At serving time, stir in toasted bread cubes and sprinkle cheese over top.
Yield: 6 servings

A Scandinavian superstition assures that "a boy and a girl" eating from the same loaf of bread will fall in love.

Scalloped Corn Sauterne

¼ cup chopped green
   pepper
2 tablespoons chopped
   onion
3 tablespoons butter or
   margarine
¼ cup flour
1 cup milk
½ cup Sauterne

1 cup grated Cheddar
   cheese
1 cup soft bread
   crumbs
1 can (12 ounces)
   whole-kernel corn,
   drained
2 eggs, slightly beaten
   Salt and pepper
   Paprika

Add green pepper and onion to melted butter in saucepan. Cook gently for 5 minutes. Blend in flour. Add milk and wine. Cook, stirring constantly, until mixture boils and thickens. Add cheese. Stir over low heat until melted. Remove from heat. Add bread crumbs, corn, eggs, and salt and pepper to taste. Pour into a greased casserole (10 x 6 x 2 inches). Sprinkle with paprika. Bake in a moderate oven (350°F.) for about 50 minutes, or until firm in center.
Yield: 6 servings

Custard Corn Pudding

3 eggs, well beaten
1 can (1 pound) cream-style
   corn
1¼ teaspoons salt
¼ teaspoon pepper
1 tablespoon instant minced
   onion
2 tablespoons fine dry
   bread crumbs

1 can (14½ ounces)
   evaporated milk,
   undiluted
⅓ cup water
2 tablespoons butter
   or margarine
   Paprika

Combine eggs, corn, salt, pepper, onion and dry bread crumbs. Put evaporated milk, water and butter in saucepan. Heat slowly until butter is melted. Add to corn and mix well. Pour into a buttered shallow

1½-quart casserole. Sprinkle with paprika. Set in a pan of warm water. Bake in a slow oven (325°F.) for about 1¼ hours, or until a knife inserted in the center comes out clean.

Yield: 6 servings

Spinach Au Gratin

1½ tablespoons flour
¼ teaspoon salt
Dash of pepper
½ teaspoon dry mustard
½ teaspoon monosodium glutamate
2 tablespoons butter or margarine
⅔ cup milk

¾ cup grated cheese, divided
1 can (15 ounces) spinach or other greens
⅓ cup fine dry bread crumbs
4 hard-cooked eggs, for garnish

Blend flour and seasonings into melted butter. Pour in milk and cook, stirring, until thickened. Add ½ cup of the cheese and the well-drained spinach. Mix. Pour into a casserole. Mix bread crumbs with remaining cheese. Sprinkle over spinach. Bake in a moderate oven (375°F.) for about 25 minutes, until crumbs are browned. Garnish with eggs, if desired.

Yield: 4 servings

Caesar's Green Beans

1 cup soft ½-inch bread cubes
3 tablespoons salad oil, divided
2 cups cooked green beans
1 tablespoon vinegar

1½ teaspoons minced onion
¼ teaspoon salt
2 tablespoons grated Parmesan cheese

Fry bread cubes in 2 tablespoons salad oil until golden. Add beans. Combine remaining salad oil, vinegar, onion and salt. Add to beans.

Heat for 10 minutes. Sprinkle with Parmesan cheese.
Yield: 4 servings

Rice N' Cheese Nibblers

⅔ cup uncooked rice
1 cup freshly grated
Cheddar cheese
1 egg, beaten
1 teaspoon salt
⅛ teaspoon pepper
½ teaspoon
Worcestershire sauce
⅛ teaspoon hot
pepper sauce

2 teaspoons prepared
horseradish
1 teaspoon minced
onion
½ teaspoon dry
mustard
¼ cup dry bread
crumbs
Oil or shortening

Cook rice according to package directions. Add cheese to hot rice and stir until melted. Combine and mix remaining ingredients except bread crumbs and oil. Stir into rice mixture. Chill for several hours or overnight. Form rice mixture into 1-inch balls. Coat thoroughly with bread crumbs. Fry in oil for 3 minutes, or until golden brown.
Yield: 3 dozen

The Biblical term "breaking bread" stems from the fact that in ancient times bread was baked in thin sheets and was actually broken by hand, never cut.

Baked Asparagus

2 packages (10 ounces
each) frozen asparagus
6 tablespoons butter or
margarine, melted,
divided

½ cup grated
Parmesan or Swiss
cheese
¼ cup dry bread
crumbs

Cook asparagus according to directions on package. Place lengthwise
in greased baking dish (8 x 12 inches). Add 5 tablespoons butter or
margarine. Sprinkle with cheese and spread with bread crumbs combined with the remaining 1 tablespoon butter. Bake in a moderate oven
(400°F.) for about 10 minutes, or until cheese is slightly melted and
crumbs browned.
Yield: 6 servings

Potato Croquettes

2 cups mashed potatoes
1 egg, beaten
1 tablespoon grated
Parmesan cheese
1 teaspoon salt
½ teaspoon pepper

2 tablespoons
chopped parsley
¾ cup dry bread
crumbs
3 tablespoons
cooking oil

Combine potatoes, egg, cheese, salt, pepper and parsley. Form into
croquettes and roll them in bread crumbs. Chill for 30 minutes. Fry
croquettes in cooking oil until brown, about 10 minutes on each side.
Yield: 4 servings

The Romans ate sandwiches (called *offula*) centuries before the Earl
of Sandwich made them popular.

Tomatoes and Mushrooms Sautés

¼ pound mushrooms,
   chopped
3 tablespoons butter,
   divided
2 tablespoons flour
⅛ teaspoon dried basil
¼ teaspoon dried orégano
2 drops of Worcestershire
   sauce
2 drops of hot pepper
   sauce

⅔ cup milk
4 medium-size
   tomatoes, peeled and
   cored
¼ teaspoon salt
¼ teaspoon pepper
¼ cup soft bread
   crumbs
4 teaspoons Parmesan
   cheese

Cook mushrooms in 2 tablespoons hot butter in 10-inch frypan over medium heat. Lower heat and simmer until tender. Blend in flour and cook for 1 minute. Add seasonings. Stir in milk gradually. Cook, stirring constantly, until thickened. Sprinkle tomatoes with salt and pepper. Fill centers with mushroom mixture. Top with bread crumbs. Dot with remaining butter. Sprinkle with cheese. Place tomatoes in frypan. Cover and cook for 5 to 8 minutes.
Yield: 4 servings

Tomato Broil

4 medium-size tomatoes
½ cup fine dry bread crumbs
½ teaspoon dried orégano
½ teaspoon salt
¼ teaspoon pepper
1 tablespoon chopped
   parsley

1 tablespoon lemon
   juice
3 tablespoons melted
   butter or margarine

Cut tomatoes crosswise into halves. Arrange in shallow baking pan. Combine dry bread crumbs, orégano, salt, pepper, parsley, lemon juice and butter. Broil tomatoes for about 3 minutes. Spread about 1 tablespoon crumb mixture over top of each tomato half. Return to broiler for 2 minutes, or until top is browned slightly.
Yield: 8 servings

Summer vegetable Rabbit

2 tablespoons butter or
 margarine
2 tablespoons flour
⅓ teaspoon salt
 Dash of cayenne
¼ teaspoon dry mustard
½ teaspoon Worcestershire
 sauce
1 cup milk
1½ cups grated American
 cheese

½ cup chopped
 cooked celery
1 tablespoon minced
 cooked green pepper
¾ cup chopped
 cooked carrot
¾ cup cooked peas
1 cup fresh tomato
 wedges
16 slices of enriched
 white bread, toasted

Melt butter in the top part of double boiler. Blend in flour, salt, cayenne, mustard and Worcestershire sauce. Add milk and cook until thick, stirring constantly. Add cheese and stir until cheese melts. Add celery, green pepper, carrot, peas and tomatoes. Cover and heat through. Serve on toast.

Yield: 8 servings, 2 slices of toast per serving

Tomatoes Milano

2 large firm tomatoes
1 cup soft bread crumbs,
 divided
1 tablespoon sugar
¼ teaspoon salt
⅛ teaspoon pepper

1 large onion, sliced
 thin
½ cup dairy sour cream
4 or 5 plum or cherry
 tomatoes, for garnish

Peel and slice large tomatoes. Place in a 1-quart casserole that has been generously buttered and sprinkled with ½ cup soft bread crumbs. Sprinkle with seasonings. Top with sliced onion. Mix the remaining ½ cup soft bread crumbs with sour cream and spread evenly over the top. Bake in a moderate oven (325°F.) for 30 minutes. At serving time slice plum or cherry tomatoes and arrange slices around inside edge of casserole for garnish.

Yield: 4 to 6 servings

Casserole Aux Champignons

1 cup soft ½-inch bread
  cubes
2 cups sliced mushrooms
1 cup grated sharp cheese
½ cup chopped celery
2 tablespoons minced onion

2 eggs, beaten
¾ teaspoon dry mustard
½ teaspoon salt
⅛ teaspoon pepper
1½ cups milk

Arrange layers of bread cubes, mushrooms, cheese, celery and onion in a greased 1-quart casserole. Combine beaten eggs, mustard, salt, pepper and milk. Pour over bread in casserole. Bake in a moderate oven (325°F.) for 1 hour.
Yield: 6 to 8 servings

Vegetable Fondue

1 quart soft ½-inch bread
  cubes
2 cups grated sharp cheese
½ cup shelled peas
½ cup diced carrots
½ cup whole-kernel corn
½ cup cut green beans

½ cup chopped celery
¼ cup grated onion
4 eggs
2 cups milk
1 teaspoon salt
¼ teaspoon pepper

Combine bread cubes, cheese, peas, carrots, corn, beans, celery and onion in a greased 3-quart casserole. Beat eggs slightly. Add milk, salt and pepper. Pour liquid mixture over bread and vegetables. Bake in a moderate oven (350°F.) for 1 hour.
Yield: 8 servings

To all his other titles King Henry IV of France added "King of Bread" because he believed that "he who rules the nation's bread is a greater ruler than he who rules its citizens' souls."

Parma Croquettes

3 slices of enriched white
    bread (1 or 2 days old)
2 eggs
⅔ cup milk
¼ teaspoon garlic salt

1 tablespoon chopped
    parsley
1 cup fine-grated
    Parmesan cheese

Cut bread into ½-inch cubes. Beat eggs. Add milk, garlic salt, parsley and Parmesan cheese. Using a slotted spoon, coat bread cubes with egg-cheese mixture. French fry in hot deep fat (375°F. on a frying thermometer) until golden brown. Serve as a top garnish for soup and salad. Yield: 6 to 8 servings

Broiled Apple Rounds

24 slices of enriched white
    bread, toasted
½ cup butter or margarine,
    softened
24 slices of bacon, chopped

24 small slices of cored
    apples, ½ inch thick
¾ pound process
    American cheese,
    grated

With a cookie cutter cut a 3-inch circle from each slice of toast. Butter toast rounds. Fry chopped bacon until crisp. Sauté apple slices on both sides in bacon fat. Place apple slices on toast rounds. Combine bacon with cheese and sprinkle over apples. Place on a greased cookie sheet and toast under medium broiler heat for 2 minutes, or until cheese melts.
Yield: 24 apple rounds

The Greeks once believed it sinful to take two bites of food in succession without a mouthful of bread in between.

Marinated Asparagus Rolls

24 green asparagus tips,
cooked and drained
¼ cup French dressing
24 slices of enriched
white bread

¾ cup Danish Blue-
cheese spread
Dash of paprika

Marinate asparagus in French dressing. Spread bread slices with cheese spread. Sprinkle with paprika. Trim crusts from bread. Place bread slices in a colander in a single layer, cheese side up. Stand colander over boiling water, but do not allow water to touch bread. Steam bread until it just begins to feel moist on underside. Remove bread from colander. Place an asparagus tip on top of cheese at one end of each bread slice and immediately roll up like a jelly roll. Place on a cookie sheet so that roll rests on last turn of bread. Toast under medium broiler heat (425°F.) for 3 minutes, or until golden brown.
Yield: 24 asparagus rolls

Corny Filled Peppers

6 green peppers
¼ cup butter or margarine
¼ cup minced onion
4 eggs, beaten
2 cups cooked corn kernels
⅔ cup heavy cream
½ teaspoon salt

¼ teaspoon pepper
Few grains of grated
nutmeg
Few grains of cayenne
2 tablespoons ketchup
½ cup dry bread crumbs
½ teaspoon paprika

Wash peppers. Cut off stems and remove fibers and seeds. Place upright in greased 1½-quart baking dish. Melt butter or margarine. Add onion. Sauté until golden. Combine remaining ingredients except paprika; mix well. Fill peppers with mixture. Sprinkle paprika on top. Bake in moderate oven (325°F.) for 45 minutes.
Yield: 6 servings

In Morocco, stale bread is considered excellent for curing stuttering.

HOT SANDWICHES

Applesauce Frenchies

2 cups canned applesauce
½ teaspoon ground
    cinnamon
½ teaspoon grated nutmeg
1 tablespoon butter
2 eggs

1⅓ cups milk
    Few grains of salt
8 slices of enriched
    white bread
    Butter or margarine

Combine applesauce, spices and butter. Heat. Beat eggs. Add milk and salt. Dip bread slices into egg mixture. Brown on both sides in butter or margarine to make French toast. Serve hot applesauce mixture between 2 slices of French toast. If desired, garnish tops with spoonfuls of applesauce.

Yield: 4 servings

Stretchies

1 pound ground beef
½ pound pork sausage meat
1 egg
⅛ teaspoon garlic salt
½ teaspoon celery salt
1 teaspoon salt
⅛ teaspoon pepper
¼ teaspoon dried orégano
¾ cup fine dry bread
 crumbs
⅓ cup water

1 can (8 ounces) pizza
 sauce
1 cup sliced or slivered
 black or green olives
1 can (4 ounces)
 mushroom pieces
¾ cup grated
 mozzarella cheese
12 frankfurter buns,
 split and heated

Combine beef, sausage, egg, garlic salt, celery salt, salt, pepper, orégano, dry bread crumbs and water. Blend thoroughly. Place meat mixture on a shallow baking pan, then spread it out into an oblong about 15 x 6 inches. Bake in a moderate oven (350°F.) for 25 minutes. Remove from oven and drain off excess fat. Top meat with pizza sauce, olives, mushrooms and cheese. Return to oven and bake for another 10 minutes. To serve, cut meat into 12 equal sized strips and insert into hot frankfurter buns. Serve immediately.
Yield: 6 to 12 servings

Bubbly Burgers

⅓ cup smoky cheese spread
1 tablespoon minced onion,
 divided
½ cup soft bread crumbs
½ teaspoon salt

⅛ teaspoon pepper
¼ cup milk
1 egg, slightly beaten
1 pound ground beef
6 hamburger buns, split

Combine cheese spread and 1 teaspoon onion. Combine soft bread crumbs, salt, pepper, remaining 2 teaspoons onion, milk, beaten egg and beef. Form into 6 patties, using about ⅓ cup of mixture for each one. Make a well in the center of each patty by pressing center with the back of tablespoon. Place on a moderately hot greased (350°F.) griddle with the "well" side turned down. When browned on under side, turn and fill "well" with about 1 tablespoon of the cheese mixture. Continue until browned on second side. Toast cut surfaces of buns on grill. To serve, place a hamburger in each toasted bun.

Yield: 3 to 6 servings

Asparagus Soufflé Sandwich

2 tablespoons soft butter or
   margarine
6 slices of enriched white
   bread
18 asparagus stalks, cooked
½ teaspoon salt
3 eggs, separated
   Dash of pepper

⅛ teaspoon paprika
½ teaspoon
   Worcestershire sauce
½ teaspoon prepared
   mustard
¾ cup grated sharp
   cheese

Spread butter on bread slices. Place 3 asparagus stalks on each slice. Add salt to egg whites and beat until stiff but not dry. Add pepper, paprika, Worcestershire sauce and mustard to egg yolks and beat until light. Add cheese. Fold egg-yolk and cheese mixture into stiffly beaten egg whites. Top each asparagus sandwich with about ⅓ cup soufflé mixture. Place on a greased baking sheet and bake in a moderate oven (350°F.) for 15 minutes, or until brown.

Yield: 3 to 6 servings

In order to get votes, later Roman politicians often distributed free bread to citizens.

Huevos Rancheros

¼ pound bacon
¼ cup minced onion
¼ to ½ teaspoon chopped
  dried red pepper
1 can (17 ounces) tomatoes
⅛ pound sharp Cheddar
  cheese, grated

¼ teaspoon garlic salt
Dash of black pepper
6 eggs
6 slices of enriched
  white bread, toasted

Cut bacon into ½-inch pieces. Fry in large frypan until almost crisp. Add onion and sauté. Add red pepper, tomatoes, cheese, garlic salt and black pepper. Simmer for 10 minutes, stirring constantly, making sure that cheese melts and tomatoes break into pieces. Crack eggs, dropping each one into position over tomatoes. Cover, and poach eggs for about 5 minutes. Top each slice of toast with an egg and some sauce.
Yield: 6 servings

Barbecued Beef Kabobs

2 pounds beef sirloin
2 teaspoons salt
1 teaspoon chili powder
½ teaspoon poultry
  seasoning
½ teaspoon dried orégano
½ teaspoon ground ginger
¼ teaspoon pepper
¼ teaspoon garlic
  powder

2 tablespoons minced
  fresh onion
2 tablespoons fresh
  lemon juice
1 tablespoon cider
  vinegar
½ cup salad oil
Frankfurter rolls
Grilled fresh
  vegetables

Cut beef into 1½-inch cubes and place in a bowl. Combine salt, seasonings, onion, lemon juice, vinegar and oil. Pour over beef. Marinate in refrigerator overnight, or at room temperature for 3 to 4 hours. String meat on skewers. Broil over charcoal grill for 15 to 20 minutes, turning skewers frequently to brown all sides. Baste with marinade while cooking as often as meat looks dry. Serve between split frankfurter rolls with Grilled Vegetables (see next page).

Grilled Fresh Vegetables

Peel small white onions and parboil in boiling salted water for 10 minutes, using 1 teaspoon salt to each quart of boiling water. Cut green peppers into 1½-inch strips; string on skewers alternating with parboiled onions. Cut ripe firm tomatoes into wedges; string on skewers. Place skewered vegetables over charcoal fire when the meat is about half done. Cook until vegetables are tender, basting with marinade as often as vegetables look dry. Serve with Barbecued Beef Kabobs.
Yield: allow 2 onions, 2 pieces of green pepper and 2 tomato wedges per person; 8 to 12 servings of meat

Chicken Crisp Indienne

2 cans (4¾ ounces each) chicken spread	2 eggs
12 slices of enriched white bread	1 teaspoon curry powder
⅔ cup undiluted evaporated milk	¼ teaspoon salt
	2 cups cornflakes, crushed

Spread chicken spread on 6 slices of bread and top with remaining 6 slices of bread. Place evaporated milk, eggs, curry powder and salt in a shallow dish. Beat with fork until well blended. Dip one side of each sandwich, then the other, into the egg mixture, then dip each sandwich into cornflake crumbs. Brown each side of sandwich on lightly greased hot griddle. Serve immediately.
Yield: 3 to 6 servings

At Turkish weddings the groom's mother is obliged to present every guest with a crescent roll in order to "assure good luck to the happy couple."

Triple-deck Sausage Sandwich

1 pound pork sausage
¼ cup chopped green
pepper
¼ cup chopped onion
2 tablespoons water
½ cup grated Cheddar
cheese

1 can (10¾ ounces)
condensed
mushroom soup
12 slices of enriched
white bread
3 tablespoons milk

Place sausage, green pepper, onion and water in cold frypan. Cover tightly and cook slowly for about 5 minutes. Pour off drippings and stir in grated cheese. Add ¼ cup mushroom soup and blend with sausage mixture. Remove crusts from bread. Allow 8 slices of bread for spreading with sausage mixture. Spread 1 slice of bread with filling; top with second slice. Spread second slice with filling and top with third slice. Allow about ¼ cup sausage mixture for each layer. Place on cookie sheet and brown in hot oven (400°F.) for 5 to 7 minutes. Add milk to the remaining soup. Heat and serve as a sauce over sandwiches, if desired.

Yield: 4 servings

In 1773, during a flour shortage in Sicily, bread was literally worth its weight in gold.

DESSERTS

Fig Pudding

½ cup ground figs
½ cup dry bread crumbs
¼ teaspoon vanilla extract
½ cup buttermilk
3 tablespoons melted
  margarine
1 egg, beaten
¾ cups sifted flour
½ teaspoon baking
  powder
½ teaspoon baking soda
½ teaspoon ground
  cinnamon
½ teaspoon grated
  mace
½ cup firmly packed
  brown sugar

Mix figs, bread crumbs, vanilla extract, buttermilk and melted margarine in large mixing bowl. Add egg and stir until thoroughly mixed. Sift together flour, baking powder, baking soda, cinnamon, mace and brown sugar. Add to fig mixture and stir well. Turn into a well-greased 1-quart mold or 6 individual molds. Cover molds with tight lids or aluminum foil. Set in pan of hot water, letting water come up 1 inch on sides of pudding dishes. Cover pan and steam pudding in slow oven (250°F.) for 2 hours. Serve warm or cold with Lemon Sauce*, Hard Sauce*, or both.

*Lemon Sauce

½ cup sugar
2 tablespoons cornstarch
1 cup boiling water

¼ cup lemon juice
1 teaspoon grated
lemon rind
1 tablespoon margarine

Mix sugar and cornstarch. Stir into boiling water in saucepan. Cook until thick and clear, stirring constantly. Remove from heat. Add lemon juice, rind, and margarine. Mix well.

*Hard Sauce

⅓ cup margarine
1 cup sifted confectioners'
sugar

1 teaspoon rum
flavoring
Pinch of salt

Cream margarine until light and fluffy. Add sugar gradually, continuing to stir until creamy. Add flavoring, a little at a time, and salt. Mix well. Pile into serving dish and chill.
Yield: 6 servings

In Bogliasco, Italy, bread is baked in the shape of fish, birds and snakes instead of the regular elongated loaves.

Prune Betty

⅓ cup butter or margarine
3 cups soft bread crumbs
2 cups cooked prunes
1 apple
½ cup firmly packed
  brown sugar

½ teaspoon ground
  cinnamon
½ cup cooking liquid
  from prunes
1 tablespoon lemon
  juice

Melt butter and pour over bread crumbs, tossing to mix evenly. Pit and chop prunes. Pare, core, and slice apple. Arrange layers of bread, apple and prunes in greased shallow baking dish. Sprinkle sugar and cinnamon over fruits as layers are made, ending with bread crumbs. Combine prune cooking liquid and lemon juice, and sprinkle over all. Bake in a moderate oven (375°F.) for 40 to 45 minutes, until apples are tender and top is browned. Serve warm or cold, plain or with cream.
Yield: 5 to 6 servings

Christmas Plum Pudding

1¼ cups seedless raisins
1¼ cups dried currants
½ cup chopped nutmeats
1 cup sifted flour, divided
2 eggs, beaten
¾ cup light molasses
¾ cup buttermilk
½ cup fine-chopped suet
¼ cup pineapple juice
1 cup dry bread crumbs

¾ teaspoon baking soda
¼ teaspoon ground
  cloves
¼ teaspoon ground
  allspice
¼ teaspoon ground
  cinnamon
¼ teaspoon grated
  nutmeg
¾ teaspoon salt

Combine raisins, currants, nutmeats and ½ cup flour. Combine eggs, molasses, buttermilk, suet and fruit juice. Combine remaining flour, crumbs, baking soda, spices and salt, and add to egg mixture. Add floured fruits and mix well. Pour into greased 1½-quart mold. Cover and set on a rack in a deep kettle. Add boiling water to about 1 inch below cover of mold. Cover. Steam continually for 1½ to 2 hours. Serve with Hard-Sauce Snowmen (see next page).

Hard-Sauce Snowmen

⅓ cup butter or margarine	1 teaspoon vanilla
2 cups (10x) confectioners'	extract
sugar	Whole cloves
	Candied cherries

Cream first 3 ingredients until smooth. Form into balls of 3 different sizes and put together to form snowmen. Decorate with whole cloves and bits of candied cherries.

Yield: 10 to 12 servings

Fresh Blueberry Refrigerator Pudding

⅓ cup sugar	4 slices of enriched
¼ cup water	white bread
1 pint fresh blueberries	2 tablespoons soft
2 teaspoons lemon juice	butter or margarine
1½ teaspoons cornstarch	½ cup heavy cream,
1½ tablespoons cold	whipped
water	

Combine sugar and ¼ cup water. Cook, stirring constantly, to boiling. Add berries and simmer for 3 to 4 minutes. Stir in lemon juice and corn-starch blended with 1½ tablespoons cold water. Cook, stirring con-stantly, until thickened. Remove from heat. Cool to lukewarm. Line a loaf pan (9 x 5 inches) with wax paper. Trim crusts from bread; spread with butter or margarine. Cut each slice into quarters. Place half of bread slices in bottom of prepared pan, buttered side up. Spread with half of berry mixture. Top with remaining bread and spread with re-maining berry mixture. Cover with wax paper and store in refrigerator for 2 to 3 hours, or overnight. When ready to serve, remove from pan. Spread top and sides with whipped cream. Slice and serve.

Yield: 4 servings

A loaf of Arab bread is as thin as cardboard and a half a yard in diameter.

Pain Perdu

2 eggs
½ cup sugar
½ teaspoon grated lemon
    rind
1 cup milk

1 teaspoon vanilla
    extract
8 slices dried bread
2 tablespoons butter

Beat eggs with sugar. Stir in lemon rind, milk and vanilla, and blend. Pour over bread slices in shallow dish. Let soak for 30 minutes. Preheat large frypan over medium heat. Add butter. When melted, add bread slices. Fry until brown, about 6 minutes on each side. Sprinkle with powdered sugar and/or nutmeg. Serve with preserves or cane syrup.
Yield: 4 servings

Creole Bread Pudding

⅓ loaf of dried French
    bread, cut into ½-inch
    cubes
¼ cup raisins
2 tablespoons butter
2 eggs, separated

10 tablespoons sugar,
    divided
1¼ cups milk
1 teaspoon vanilla
    extract
¼ teaspoon cream of
    tartar

Moisten bread cubes with water; squeeze dry. Mix with raisins and butter in 1-quart dish. Beat egg yolks with 6 tablespoons sugar; stir in milk until smooth. Add vanilla. Pour liquid over bread cubes. Bake in moderate oven (350°F.) for 45 minutes. Beat egg whites until foamy. Add cream of tartar. Gradually add remaining 4 tablespoons sugar. Beat until stiff but not dry. Spoon on top of pudding. Brown in moderate oven (350°F.) for 12 to 15 minutes.
Yield: 4 servings

At one time Arabian princes ratified treaties by sprinkling salt on a piece of bread.

Florida Sunshine Pudding

3 cups fine soft bread
crumbs
¾ cup minced or ground
suet
1 tablespoon grated orange
rind
½ teaspoon ground
cinnamon
¼ teaspoon ground cloves

¼ teaspoon grated
mace
1 cup orange
marmalade
2 eggs, well beaten
½ teaspoon baking soda
⅓ cup orange juice
1 tablespoon
granulated sugar

Combine soft bread crumbs and suet. Blend orange rind, cinnamon, cloves and mace with marmalade. Add beaten eggs to marmalade mixture. Dissolve baking soda in orange juice. Add to egg mixture and combine with bread-crumb mixture. Sprinkle sugar over inside of a well-buttered 1-quart pudding mold. Pour pudding into sugared mold and cover tightly. Place on a rack in boiling water. Cover and steam for 2½ to 3 hours, or until a wooden pick inserted in center of pudding comes out clean. Serve hot with Orange Hard Sauce*.

*Orange Hard Sauce

⅓ cup soft butter or
margarine
1¼ cups confectioners' sugar
Dash of salt

½ teaspoon grated
orange rind
1 tablespoon orange
juice

Cream butter, sugar and salt until soft and smooth. Add orange rind and juice. Beat well. Chill in refrigerator.
Yield: 8 to 10 servings

Physicians of ancient Egypt pronounced their patients cured if they could eat without discomfort a whole loaf of bread and a chicken.

Bread and Butter Pudding

4 slices of buttered bread,
quartered
½ cup sugar, divided
1 package (5 ounces)
vanilla pudding and
pie filling

4 cups milk
½ cup raisins
½ teaspoon grated
nutmeg

Place bread in a baking dish (8 x 8 x 2 inches). Sprinkle with ¼ cup sugar. Combine remaining sugar, pudding mix, milk and raisins in 3-quart saucepan. Cook over medium heat, stirring constantly, until mixture boils. Pour over bread. Sprinkle with nutmeg. Serve warm.
Yield: 6 to 8 servings

Applesauce-Pineapple Muffins

1 quart ½-inch soft bread
cubes
4 teaspoons butter or
margarine
4 teaspoons minced onion
¾ teaspoon salt

Dash of pepper
¾ cup applesauce
½ cup drained
pineapple tidbits
3 tablespoons brown
sugar

Spread out bread cubes in a shallow pan. Heat in a moderate oven (350°F.) until toasted, turning frequently. Melt butter in a small frypan. Add onion and sauté until tender. Combine toasted bread cubes, sautéed onion, salt, pepper, applesauce and pineapple in a 2-quart bowl. Place about ⅓ cup mixture in each lined muffin cup. Sprinkle 1 teaspoon brown sugar over each. Bake in a moderate oven (350°F.) until browned, or 20 to 25 minutes.
Yield: 8 muffins

In the Middle Ages, if a suspected criminal could not swallow a piece of dry holy bread and some cheese, he was pronounced guilty.

Praline Toast

6 tablespoons butter
1 cup firmly packed light
  brown sugar
¼ cup undiluted
  evaporated milk

⅔ cup sliced pecans
10 slices of enriched
  white bread

Melt butter and stir in sugar, evaporated milk and pecans. Toast bread on one side under broiler. Spread untoasted side with pecan mixture. Broil again until bubbly and hot, 1 to 2 minutes.
Yield: 5 to 10 servings

Steamed Pumpkin Bread Pudding

1¼ cups fine dry bread
  crumbs
½ cup sifted enriched flour
1 teaspoon baking powder
½ teaspoon salt
½ teaspoon baking soda
½ teaspoon ground
  cinnamon
½ teaspoon ground
  cloves

½ cup corn oil
1 cup firmly packed
  brown sugar
2 eggs
½ cup undiluted
  evaporated milk
1½ cups canned
  pumpkin

In large mixing bowl combine dry bread crumbs with flour, baking powder, salt, baking soda, cinnamon and cloves. Blend corn oil, brown sugar and eggs together. Beat well. Add flour mixture, alternately with evaporated milk and pumpkin, to creamed mixture. Fill a large well-greased pudding mold two-thirds full of pudding mixture. Using foil, cover container tightly. Steam for 2½ to 3 hours, or until a wooden pick inserted in center comes out clean. Cool slightly and remove from mold. Serve warm with Lemon-Nut Sauce (see next page).

In Colonial times a loaf of freshly baked bread was sniffed for the relief of head colds.

Lemon-Nut Sauce

2 cups sifted confectioners' sugar	½ cup butter or margarine
¼ teaspoon salt	½ cup chopped walnuts
¼ teaspoon ground ginger	¼ cup lemon juice

Combine confectioners' sugar, salt and ginger. Beat sugar mixture into butter, adding 2 tablespoons at a time. When light, add chopped walnuts. Add lemon juice slowly to prevent curdling.

Yield: 10 to 12 servings

Swiss Apple Pie

¼ cup butter or margarine	4 cups thin-sliced tart apples
1½ cups sifted all-purpose flour	2 whole eggs
3 tablespoons cold water (about)	2 extra egg yolks
1 tablespoon crushed toasted almonds	2 cups heavy cream
1 tablespoon fine dry bread crumbs	¾ cup sugar, divided
	2 tablespoons butter or margarine, melted

Cut butter into flour with pastry blender or 2 knives. Add cold water gradually, mixing with fork, until pastry gathers around fork. Roll out on lightly floured board into a sheet ⅛ inch thick. Line a deep 10-inch pie pan, layering evenly. Trim edge. Sprinkle almonds and crumbs over pastry in bottom of pie pan. (Do not heap.) Bake in a moderate oven (350°F.) for 5 minutes. Arrange apple slices evenly over the partly baked pastry.

Meanwhile combine whole eggs and extra yolks. Beat slightly. Add cream and ½ cup sugar. Stir until sugar dissolves. Pour half of this mixture over apples. Bake for about 30 minutes, until custard is firm. Pour in remaining mixture. Bake again for about 30 minutes, until a knife inserted near edge comes out clean. Remove pie from oven. Pour melted butter evenly over top. Sprinkle with remaining ¼ cup sugar. Return to oven. Bake for 5 minutes longer, or until top is crusty and golden. Let pie cool somewhat before cutting.

Yield: 6 to 8 servings

Danish Apple Pudding

6 slices of enriched white
  bread
¼ cup butter or margarine
½ cup sugar

1 can (1 pound)
  applesauce
½ cup heavy cream,
  whipped
Preserves or jam

Tear bread into crumbs (about 3 cups). Combine butter and sugar in frypan. Heat until well blended, stirring constantly. Add crumbs, stirring until they are coated with the mixture and lightly browned. Put half of crumbs in a layer-cake pan. Spread with applesauce and top with remaining crumbs. Chill for several hours. Serve topped with spoonfuls of whipped cream, and garnish with a bit of preserves.

Yield: 6 servings

Peach Crisp Pudding

¼ cup butter or margarine
½ cup sugar
1 quart soft ½-inch
  bread cubes

2 cups sliced peaches
Whipped cream

Cream butter and sugar together. Combine with soft bread cubes and peaches. Bake in a greased 1½-quart casserole in a moderate oven (375°F.) for 30 minutes. Serve with whipped cream.

Yield: 8 servings

In Montenegro men could once divorce wives who didn't know how to bake bread.

Upside-down Apple Pudding

2 tablespoons melted butter
or margarine
⅓ cup firmly packed
brown sugar
2 cups pared raw apple
slices
2 eggs, slightly beaten

¼ cup milk
⅛ teaspoon ground
cloves
⅛ teaspoon salt
1 cup apple butter
1 quart toasted ½-inch
bread cubes

Spread half of the butter in the bottom of a 1½-quart casserole. Sprinkle about half of the brown sugar over the butter. Arrange apple slices on top of brown sugar. Combine beaten eggs, milk, cloves, salt, apple butter and remaining melted butter. Add toasted bread cubes. Arrange bread-cube mixture over apple slices. Bake in a moderate oven (350°F.) for 40 minutes, or until apples are tender. Remove from oven and let pudding stand for a few minutes. Then invert onto a serving plate so apple slices are on top. Immediately sprinkle remaining brown sugar over top of pudding. Serve warm, with light cream if desired.

Yield: 8 servings

Finland Pudding

1½ tablespoons brown sugar
1½ teaspoons flour
3 teaspoons grated orange
rind, divided
3 tablespoons orange juice,
divided
½ teaspoon salt
1 pint blueberries

2 cups ¼-inch bread
cubes, toasted
1 egg
3 tablespoons brown
sugar
¾ cup crushed vanilla
wafers
Sour cream

Combine brown sugar, flour, 2 teaspoons orange rind, 2 tablespoons orange juice and salt. Add blueberries and toasted bread cubes. Pour into a greased 1-quart casserole. Beat egg slightly, and add brown sugar and remaining orange rind and juice. Stir in vanilla wafers. Spread

topping evenly over berry mixture. Bake in a moderate oven (350°F.) for 25 minutes. Serve warm with sour cream.
Yield: 6 servings

Cider Torte

4 eggs, separated
1 cup sugar
1¼ teaspoons dehydrated lemon rind
¾ teaspoon ground cinnamon
2⅔ cups toasted medium-fine bread crumbs

⅔ cup toasted fine-chopped almonds
2½ to 3 cups sweet apple cider
1 cup heavy cream, whipped

Beat egg whites until foamy. Gradually beat in half of the sugar and continue beating until very stiff and shiny. Beat egg yolks until thick, and until color changes to light yellow. Slowly add remaining sugar, beating well after each addition. Add lemon rind and cinnamon. Gently fold in bread crumbs and almonds, then beaten egg whites. Spoon into a well-greased 8-inch tube pan lined with wax paper. Bake in a moderate (350°F.) oven for 45 to 50 minutes, or until set and lightly browned. Heat cider and slowly pour half of it over top of *Torte*. Remove *Torte* from pan and place upside down on a plate. Immediately peel off paper. Pour just enough of remaining cider over *Torte* to saturate it. Top each serving with whipped cream.
Yield: 16 servings

To announce that their bread was ready for sale, 14th-century bakers blew loud blasts on horns.

Date-Nut Pudding

¼ cup soft butter or
  margarine
½ cup sugar
1 teaspoon vanilla extract
½ teaspoon salt
2 eggs, beaten
¼ cup milk

1½ quarts soft ½-inch
  bread cubes
2 teaspoons baking
  powder
1 cup chopped pitted
  dates
½ cup chopped walnuts

Combine butter, sugar, vanilla and salt. Add beaten eggs and milk. Combine soft bread cubes and baking powder and add to first mixture. Add dates and walnuts. Grease 7 individual 6-ounce fruit-juice cans on insides and put ¾ cup pudding mixture into each can. Cover tops with aluminum foil and press them down over sides of cans. Put 2 cups water in pressure cooker. Place cans on rack in cooker and cover cooker. Steam pudding for 15 minutes. Close steam valve and pressure-cook pudding for 30 minutes. Let pudding cool for 5 minutes before loosening with spatula and turning it out. Serve with Foamy Sauce*.

*Foamy Sauce

⅛ teaspoon salt
1 egg, separated
¼ cup brown sugar, divided

¼ teaspoon vanilla
  extract
¼ cup heavy cream,
  whipped

Add salt to egg white and beat until foamy. Sift brown sugar and gradually add 2 tablespoons sugar to the egg white, beating until mixture is well blended and egg white is stiff. Add remaining sugar and vanilla extract to egg yolk and beat until fluffy. Combine both mixtures and fold in whipped cream.
Yield: 7 individual puddings; 1½ cups sauce

The European "napkins" of the 12th century were made of dough. After they became soaked with wine and soup they were eaten by the diners.

Lemon Bread Pudding

1 package (3⅝ ounces)
lemon pudding or pie
filling
2 eggs, separated
¼ cup granulated sugar
½ teaspoon vanilla extract

3 cups soft bread
crumbs
⅓ cup firmly packed
brown sugar
⅓ cup flaked coconut
¼ cup melted butter
or margarine

Prepare pudding according to package directions, using 2 egg yolks in pudding. Beat 2 egg whites until foamy. Gradually add granulated sugar and beat until peaks form. Fold vanilla extract and meringue into cooked pudding. Pour into a 1½-quart baking dish. Combine soft bread crumbs, brown sugar and coconut. Sprinkle over pudding mixture. Drizzle melted butter over topping mixture. Bake in a moderate oven (350°F.) until topping is lightly browned, about 15 minutes.
Yield: 6 to 8 servings

Apricot-Coconut Pudding

4 slices of enriched white
bread
2 teaspoons butter or
margarine
1¾ cups apricot halves
3 eggs, beaten
¾ cup milk

¼ cup apricot juice
3 tablespoons sugar
¼ teaspoon lemon
extract
1 tablespoon shredded
coconut

Trim crusts from bread. Spread ½ teaspoon butter on each slice of bread and cut into quarters. Alternate layers of bread and apricots in a greased 1-quart casserole. Beat eggs and combine with milk, apricot juice, sugar and lemon extract. Pour over bread and apricots. Sprinkle coconut over apricots on top layer of casserole. Bake in a moderate oven (350°F.) for 50 minutes.
Yield: 6 servings

Peach Meringue Bread Pudding

2 cups soft ½-inch bread
  cubes
2 cups sliced peeled
  peaches
2 eggs, separated
1¼ cups milk
¼ teaspoon ground
  cinnamon
¼ teaspoon salt

⅛ teaspoon grated nutmeg
½ teaspoon vanilla
  extract
¼ cup firmly packed
  brown sugar
6 tablespoons
  granulated sugar,
  divided

Combine soft bread cubes and peaches in a greased 1½-quart casserole. Beat egg yolks and combine with milk, cinnamon, salt, nutmeg, vanilla extract, brown sugar and ¼ cup granulated sugar. Pour liquid mixture over bread and peaches. Bake in a moderate oven (350°F.) for 45 minutes. Remove from oven. Beat egg whites until stiff. Add remaining 2 tablespoons granulated sugar gradually, continuing to beat until mixture stands in peaks. Spread meringue over top of pudding and return to oven for 15 minutes, or until browned.
Yield: 8 servings

In the 17th century, it was customary for a Bulgarian bridegroom to carry a loaf of fresh bread to the altar to signify that he would povide well for his wife.

Holiday Steamed Pudding

1½ cups enriched all-purpose
flour
1 tablespoon baking
powder
½ cup sugar
1 teaspoon salt
1 cup butter or margarine
1½ quarts coarse soft bread
crumbs
1 tablespoon grated orange
rind

½ cup slivered candied
cherries
1½ cups slivered or
diced mixed
candied fruits
1 cup milk
2 eggs, well beaten
½ teaspoon almond
extract
¼ teaspoon grated
nutmeg

Sift flour, baking powder, sugar and salt into a large bowl. Cut in the butter with a pastry blender or 2 knives. Add soft bread crumbs, orange rind, cherries and fruits. Beat milk and eggs together. Add almond extract and nutmeg. Combine both mixtures and blend well. Pour half of batter into each of 2 well-greased 2-quart ring molds. Cover tightly. Place each on a rack in a deep kettle, filling the kettles with enough water to come halfway up sides of molds. Cover the kettles. Steam for 3 hours, adding more water if necessary. Remove from steamer and let stand for about 5 minutes. Remove covers and turn onto hot platters. Serve with hot Lemon-Nutmeg Sauce*.

*Lemon-Nutmeg Sauce

1 egg
1 cup sugar
½ teaspoon grated nutmeg
2 tablespoons grated lemon
rind

¼ cup lemon juice
3 tablespoons water
¼ cup butter

Beat egg. Add sugar, nutmeg and lemon rind. Combine lemon juice and water. Add to sugar mixture. Heat until boiling, stirring constantly. Add butter. Cook for 5 minutes, stirring until butter blends evenly into sauce. Serve hot over pudding.
Yield: 16 to 20 servings

Index